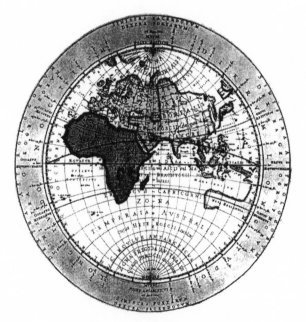

Call to Me, and I will answer you, and
show you great and mighty things,
which you do not know.
Jeremiah 33:3

BOYS OF GRIT

BY

ARCHER WALLACE

Lamplighter Publishing
Waverly, Pennsylvania

Boys of Grit Who Changed the World.

Published by Lamplighter Publishing; a division of
Cornerstone Family Ministries, Inc.

The Lamplighter Rare Collector's Series is a series
of family Christian literature from the 17th, 18th,
19th, & 20th centuries. Each edition is printed in an
attractive hard-bound collector's format. For more
information, write: Lamplighter Publishing, P.O.
Box 777, Waverly, PA 18471 or call 1-888-A-
GOSPEL.

Printed by Jostens in the United States of America
Arrestox 63200; gold M842; red GP427

ISBN 1-58474-031-0

BETWEEN OURSELVES

A FEW years ago I became convinced that many of the bravest and best people I knew had been facing difficulties all their lives, and that these very difficulties had helped them to develop muscle and backbone. In order to share this thought with boys, I wrote a book entitled *Stories of Grit,* which told, among others, the story of blind Henry Fawcett who became Post-master General of England; of a Gypsy boy born in a tent whose life has been a blessing to tens of thousands; of Booker T. Washington, a slave boy who became a great leader of his people and of Edward Bok, a poor immigrant boy who rose until he ranked among the greatest journalists of his generation.

This little book succeeded far beyond any expectations of mine. Scores of boys have written to me, not only from all over the American Continent and Great Britain, but from lands as far distant as India, Ceylon, Australia and China. Many of these boys are themselves fighting hard battles, sometimes against disease, poverty, or other circumstances which make their lot hard.   Nothing has ever given me more pleasure than to receive these letters and to know that the book has helped so many boys.

At the request of the publishers I have written another fifteen stories with the title *More Stories of Grit*.   Probably the men written about in this book were no braver than many of the boys who wrote to me, but they are all true stories of well-known men and I feel sure the account of their lives will encourage the boys who read this book.

ARCHER WALLACE

Toronto

CONTENTS

v

Prefatory Remarks

It is a special and memorable moment when one learns of another who has overcome overwhelming obstacles to achieve success and honor. The human spirit loves to cheer and applaud valor, heroism, perseverance, and victory. When I first read *Boys of Grit who Changed the World*, I was profoundly inspired. I learned of a blacksmith with average abilities who was able to master twenty languages because he understood the value of every spare moment. This common blacksmith became the first to promote world peace. In another account, a poor ridiculed boy believed that hardship was a necessary step to greatness. Penniless and friendless, Hans Anderson persevered and became one of the greatest authors of the 19th century. The life stories of Samuel Morse, Robert Fulton, Isaac Pitman, and Joseph Haydn are among a few of the young characters in this inspiring book that will give boys and girls hope, courage, conviction, and motivation to become all that God intends them to be.

So my friends, I invite you to travel with me across the globe and peek into the lives of children who learned the value of perseverance, who turned tragedy into triumph, weakness into strength, poverty into riches, and hopelessness into great joy. It is with confident anticipation that I publish this book, believing that it will not only plant a seed of inspiration, but will stir enough grit to the surface of a young person's life enabling him or her to rise to a level of greatness and honor that is so desperately needed for our day. For as it is written, "See a man diligent in his work? He shall stand before kings." Proverbs 22:9

Mark Hamby
Editor

BOYS OF GRIT

CHAPTER I.

An Irish Boy Who Became Canada's Greatest Merchant.

ONE day in 1847, a thirteen year old Irish boy entered the service of a dry goods merchant named Smith in the town of Portglenone, Ireland. The little fellow, whose name was Timothy Eaton, was one of a family of nine children. The father had died about the time Timothy was born, and the heavy responsibility of caring for the four boys and five girls rested upon the shoulders of the patient, hard-working mother.

Fatherless boys are seriously handicapped, but one compensation generally is that they learn to look out for themselves and Timothy Eaton learned to do this. One day some of his schoolmates teased him about his home-spun clothing, and the little fellow, standing with his back to the wall, fought the scoffers until they were satisfied. From that day he had the respect of the whole school and there were no more sneers because of his home-made clothing.

Mr. Smith, for whom Timothy began to

work, kept almost every kind of merchandise. There were dress goods, millinery, groceries, hardware, flour, feed, and medicine. The hours were long and the work hard. For some time the boy slept under the counter of the store and this was a convenient arrangement for often his day's work did not cease until past midnight and generally it was past one A.M. on Sunday mornings when he crawled into his humble bed.

Not far away was the town of Ballymena, and on market days Timothy had to be up by four o'clock in the morning in order to serve the farmers who were taking their produce to market. Because these men often drank liquor, the lad never forgot those experiences. His eyes and ears were wide open, and he resolved that if ever he had a place of business of his own he would never, under any circumstances, serve liquor.

Throughout the countryside there were many ragmen who went from house to house begging rags and then brought them to Mr. Smith's store to exchange for goods they wanted. Part of Timothy's work was to sort these rags and he soon learned to distinguish between cotton and wool. This was work which the boy disliked, especially because typhus fever and many other diseases were carried by filthy rags. More than once he wanted to give up but when he realized that if he did not complete his apprenticeship his mother would forfeit a bond of five hundred dollars, he determined to fulfil the contract.

On one occasion Timothy had to do some business at a place nine miles from Portglenone. His employer was also driving there that day and he told the lad that if he were at a certain place at a specified time he would give him a lift back. Timothy got through with his business and arrived at the spot less than half a minute late but, although he saw the lad hurrying up, Mr. Smith deliberately drove off, leaving the boy to trudge the nine miles home. This was the man's idea of teaching the boy punctuality and whatever Timothy thought of the lesson he said nothing but tucked it away in his memory.

Timothy Eaton completed his apprenticeship at a time when conditions in Ireland were very bad. There was distress and poverty everywhere and even hard-working, ambitious men, could scarcely earn enough to keep body and soul together. All Timothy's brothers and sisters, with one exception, had emigrated to Canada and they wrote back to Ireland telling of the greater opportunities and freedom to be found in the land of their adoption. Timothy took the five hundred dollars he had earned during the five years of his apprentice-ship, together with the silver watch that Mr. Smith gave him, and set sail for Canada.

His first position in Canada was in a village store at Glen Williams; later he moved to Kirkton with two sisters, where he began his first business venture, a general country store combined with the local post office. After getting experience in this way he joined his brother James in a dry goods and millinery store at the town of St. Mary's. He remained there for eight years and by his energy and good sense, steadily built up a fine business. During this period he was married and began a home of his own.

In 1868 Timothy and his brother James dissolved partnership, James deciding to remain in St. Mary's while Timothy moved to the city of Toronto. At that time Toronto had a population of 70,000, less than ten per cent of what it has to-day, but few people realized that it was destined to become so great a city. Timothy Eaton was just thirty-five when in 1869 he bought the small retail business of Mr. Jennings at the corner of Queen and Yonge streets. The deal was trans-acted at Mr. Jennings' home, 17 Maitland Street, and the following morning at eight o'clock Timothy Eaton took down the shutters and the T. Eaton Company was born.

At that time there was no such thing as a fixed price in business; buying was done by the barter system. When a storekeeper asked a certain price for an article he did not expect to get it and the customer had no intention of taking the first price seriously. The price asked was simply a starting-point for the bartering. Shopping was a tiresome game and a battle of wits to see who could get the better of the deal. Again the storekeeper was rarely paid with real money. He generally received farm produce which he in turn had to sell for cash. The young Irish storekeeper had long been convinced that these methods of doing business were good neither for the customer nor the merchant.

His first newspaper advertisement appeared on December 8, 1869, and announced the purchase of the business from Mr. Jennings. There was also the startling announcement that *Goods would be sold for cash only* and, furthermore, there would be *One fixed price for everything.*

The advertisement caused great astonishment. This was followed by amusement and some ridicule. The system of bartering and exchanging goods had existed so long that no one seemed to think a business could succeed by other methods. Experienced men asked who the young Irish upstart was who imagined he could change a people's habits overnight. They predicted that in a few months his business would fail; others said it could only be a matter of weeks.

Timothy Eaton was not discouraged by these predictions. He knew the bartering system of doing business was dishonest. With a fixed price, even a child could do business. All that was needed was the money and a description of the article required and the child would be treated as fairly as any grown-up person. The new store soon forged ahead. Purchasers compared the prices in Eaton's store with those elsewhere and the advantage was generally with the Irishman.

In those days whenever a customer entered a store he was almost compelled to make a purchase whether it satisfied him or no. If he hesitated he would be coaxed, implored and even bullied and insulted. If he did actually make his escape without buying anything he was made to feel like a whipped dog running away. Timothy Eaton decided to change all this. He instructed his salesclerks to be polite and obliging, to do all they could to meet the needs of customers, but not to bully anyone into buying. The natural result was that people were not afraid to enter the store and inspect goods. Soon the Eaton store was the best filled place of business in the city.

Mr. Eaton's mind was always open to receive new ideas. He was more than willing to listen to any one who had a suggestion to make. His biographer, Mr. George G. Nasmith, truly says: "If Timothy Eaton were living to-day he would be abreast or ahead of the times and would accept the most advanced ideas if they would increase the efficiency of his business."

One day when the store had become quite large, Mr. Eaton saw a big Irishman at work whom he had not seen before. "How long have you been here?" he asked. "None of your business," replied the man, who did not recognize him. "But what are you doing?" Mr. Eaton continued. The man said: "I am minding my own business and I would advise you to mind yours. Get along and don't block the passage." Mr. Eaton was very much amused and he said in his good-natured way: "That man is quite right. I wish I had five hundred men who would mind their own business and make everybody else mind his."

The Eaton business continued to grow steadily, even rapidly. In 1870 there were four employees; 1874, fourteen; in 1876, twenty-five; and in 1881, forty-eight. For several years Mr. Eaton, like other business men, did all his own buying but in 1880 he showed his confidence in the good judgment of his salesmen by sending them abroad to buy for the firm. He selected his employees with great care, then placed them in positions of trust and responsibility which put them on their mettle.

In 1884 the first Eaton catalogue was issued. It was a small booklet of thirty-two pages, but it was the beginning of the large and attractive volume which is now gotten out every year. In 1886 the first elevator was installed. It cost eleven hundred dollars and proved such an attraction to customers that one morning an order was issued that passengers would only be carried upstairs—they must walk down; this order, however, was soon rescinded.

Timothy Eaton became convinced that he would soon have to manufacture much of the goods sold in the store, so in 1886 a small factory for the making of window blinds was established. This move was quickly followed by the establishment of other factories until to-day the Eaton factory and work rooms in

Toronto alone give employment to over four thousand people.

The growth of the Timothy Eaton business has been the greatest success of its kind in the history of Canada. Branches have been opened in dozens of other cities beside Toronto and there are few commercial enterprises anywhere in the world to compare with it. The high sense of honor and love of fair play which marked Mr. Eaton have remained a tradition in the business.

Mr. Eaton died on the last day of January 1907. Forty-seven years after he arrived in Canada, an unknown Irish lad, the great merchant was laid to rest amid a nation's mourning. As soon as the news of his death was made known, messages of sympathy and respect began to pour in from all over the world until thousands of messages had been received, one from Earl Grey, the Governor General of Canada.

Timothy Eaton did a very difficult and unusual thing. He became a nation's most successful merchant and at the same time retained the respect and the admiration, even of his business rivals. Born in humble circumstances, one of nine children, fatherless from his birth, by his honesty, consideration for others and energy he left an example which will inspire ambitious boys in every country.

CHAPTER II.

NEITHER LAMENESS NOR MISFORTUNE COULD CRUSH HIS SPIRIT.

NO boy ever loved to romp about in the open air more than Walter Scott. He was born on August 15, 1771, in Edinburgh, Scotland, and for the first eighteen months of his life, was as healthy as a child could be. Then he was stricken with a fever which lasted several days and left him crippled for life. His parents tried every remedy they could think of and they sought advice in every direction but without avail.

His grandfather, Dr. Rutherford, advised that Walter should live with him in the country and take as much exercise in the open air as possible; so it was that the lame boy went to his grandfather's house at Sandy-Knowe. Dr. Rutherford said that if Walter could be swathed in the skin of a freshly killed sheep it might cure his lameness. This was done, and one of Walter's earliest recollections was that of seeing an old man, with white hair, dragging his watch along the carpet while he painfully crawled after it.

Walter became a great favorite among the kind folk of the heather-covered hills. He had a lovely Shetland pony, no bigger than a Saint Bernard dog, and so affectionate that it followed him into the house and came to him instantly when he called. When he was very small he was carried out and laid upon the rocks where his wondering eyes watched the sheep as they nibbled the grass nearby. The lovely sheep dogs, for which Scotland is famous, soon came to know the little cripple and licked his face as he gurgled with delight. As he grew older the little fellow sometimes became impatient with his shrunken leg and tried to run with his animal friends but, while he was unable to do this, life in the open air made him a sturdy child besides helping him to become one of the greatest lovers of animals who ever lived.

He was fond of roaming among the Scottish hills and listening to the tales of the simple-minded folk. He had a wonderful memory and read every book of romance that he could find with the result that his young head was soon filled with knowledge about the stirring scenes of Scottish history. He came to know old warriors who were only too glad to tell him of battles in which they had fought many years previously. As there were many picturesque ruins of old castles scattered over the countryside, with Flodden Field and Bannockburn not so far away, the boy's imagination was kindled and he seemed to live over again, the stirring days of old.

When he heard a story, or listened to one being read, he seemed to forget everything and live over the scenes. Once when his mother was reading aloud a letter she had received, telling of a shipwreck, he became agitated and excited. He lifted his hands and wildly shouted: "There's the mast gone! Crash it goes! They will all perish." On another occasion an uncle took him to see Shakespeare's play: "As You Like It." It was a marvellous experience for him and he was so completely carried away with it that, when Orlando and his brother quarrelled in the first act, Walter screamed out: "What are they quarrelling for; aren't they brothers?"

Often he was asked to read aloud or tell the stories which thrilled him and when he did so he became so excited that his listeners could not help laughing. This discomfited him as he was a sensitive boy and could not stand ridicule. Walter's mother used to say that if he had not been a cripple he would have been a soldier; this would have been a great calamity and loss to the whole world so, after all, his handicap was a blessing in disguise.

When he was seventeen Walter Scott was sent to a High School in Edinburgh. About this period of his life he says: "I did not make any great figure at High School—any exertions I made were desultory and little to be depended upon." The truth is that there were some subjects which he disliked, and never seemed to master, but the great amount of reading he had done stood him in good stead and his knowledge of Scottish history and folk-lore greatly astonished his schoolmates and teachers. Later he studied law and in 1792, when he was twenty-one, he was admitted to the Faculty of Advocates.

His heart was not in this profession; he wanted to write romantic novels about Scottish history. He said law was: "A dry and barren wilderness of forms and conveyances." He had lived so much in the glorious free open-air, roaming over the heather-covered hills with dogs, and sheep, and ponies for companions, that confinement in an office did not suit him. Fortunately he was appointed Sheriff-Deputy of Selkirkshire, a position which left him enough leisure time to turn his attention to the writing he so loved.

Walter Scott had been first an eager listener

then later a first-class teller of stories. "I was a much brighter figure on the playground than in class," he said. He was not a dunce—although one of his teachers told him that he was—but a boy who loved to gather other lads around him and stir their imaginations by his vivid descripton of battles and romantic scenes. He could not join in the school games but generally he found other boys who were not playing and to them, he would say, "Come away, and I'll tell ye a story." Now the time had come in his life when he was able to write to his heart's content.

For twenty-five years Walter Scott wrote novels and poems dealing with Scottish history; charming books which made him famous the world over. His poetry was good; his prose stories were much better. First came "Waverley" followed by "Guy Mannering;" "The Antiquary;" "The Black Dwarf;" "Old Mortality;" "Rob Roy," and "The Heart of Midlothian." Soon Walter Scott was the most famous British man of letters and through the enormous sale of his books, a wealthy man.

In 1811 he bought a farm on the banks of the river Tweed near Melrose, built a cottage upon it, and gradually enlarged and beautified the estate, which he named Abbotsford. The house itself was made beautiful without and

within. The imposing rooms were encircled
with suits of armor, swords, spears, and all
manner of flags and relics. Magnificent pictures adorned the walls. Abbotsford was like
a great museum where every picture reminded
one of a great life and every relic recalled a
battle. The noble building was surrounded
by stately trees which stretched to where the
Tweed gently murmured on its way to the sea.

These were the happiest days of Walter
Scott's life; he seemed to have everything that
heart could wish. He surrounded himself
with his beloved dogs which almost seemed
to be human, so intelligent and affectionate
were they. The dogs were allowed in the
house; indeed they had their place in the din-
ing-room. There was *Hamlet,* noisy and
boisterous like a big mischievous boy; *Marda,*
the stag-hound, serious and dignified; *Finette,*
the pet Spaniel with silky coat; the excited
little terriers, *Pepper* and *Mustard;* all watch-
ing Scott whose every word they seemed to
understand. Every morning after breakfast,
the Master set off limping into the woods followed by his dogs, all yelping joyously and
not unfrequently joined by *Hinse,* the big grey
cat, who absolutely refused to be left behind.

Scott had a bull terrier named *Camp* and
on many a jaunt he talked to the dog as he

would to a close friend. If Scott had been away for some time the servant would say: "*Camp*, Master's coming home by the ford," or perhaps some other point would be named, and unerringly *Camp* would set off to the place mentioned. When after several years of companionship poor old *Camp* died he was buried just outside Scott's window, and Sophia his little daughter told a friend: "Papa cried all night after *Camp's* death." To-day visitors to Abbotsford are shown the places where several of Scott's dogs are buried.

The first great sorrow of Walter Scott's life was his lameness but he bravely overcame this. The second great sorrow came in 1826, when he was fifty-five years of age. It is not easy briefly to explain what happened, but it was a financial misfortune which not only left him penniless but actually involved him in great debt. He had entered into partnership with a firm of book publishers which completely collapsed. Scott was not a good business man and no one was more surprised than he when the entire savings of his life were suddenly swept away.

Scott was staggered by the blow, and it told heavily upon him. Friends offered to loan him money but he refused. His creditors were willing to accept what he could pay thus enabling him to get from under the heavy debt but he refused. He resolved to devote the remainder of his life to writing books so that he might pay off his debts. "This own right hand," he declared, "shall work it all off." It was a magnificent resolution and only a brave and honest man would have made it. He was no longer a young man and on the same day that he vowed to wipe the debt out, he wrote in his diary: "I often wish I could lie down to sleep without waking."

His liabilities amounted to over seven hundred thousand dollars. He gave up his lovely home at Abbotsford although it nearly broke his great heart to do so for there was his entire collection of magnificent pictures, the furniture and treasures of a life-time, and he loved every stone and stick, every hill and dale around the beautiful estate. To deepen his sadness the wife he loved lay dying and within a few months of removal she passed away. He hired a lodging in Edinburgh and there for several years he worked at his tremendous task with restless energy and marvellous perseverance. At the end of two years he had paid his creditors the amazing sum of two hundred thousand dollars. He toiled so hard that his tired brain partly gave out and in 1830 he was stricken with paralysis from which he never fully recovered. During these days he wrote "Guy Mannering," "Ivanhoe" and a number of other great books which bear no trace of the agony it cost the author to write them.

Sick or well he wrote. Some days his assistant begged him to rest but he refused. He could do it, he declared, and he would. Friends could not fail to see how the labor told upon him; his hair became white in a year and the anxiety sapped away his strength. Then a touching and beautiful thing happened. His grateful creditors met and passed the following resolution:

"That Sir Walter Scott be requested to accept of his furniture, plate, linens, paintings, library, and curiosities of every description, as the best means the creditors have of expressing their very high sense of the most honorable conduct, and in grateful acknowledgment for the unparalleled and most successful exertions he has made and continues to make for them."

The failing condition of his health made it necessary for him to take a rest; in October 1831, the British Government placed a ship at his disposal and he sailed for Italy. While in Italy he grew worse and pined for home. He was brought back in haste. It was a long and painful journey for him but at last he

reached London and after a short rest he was
taken to Scotland. As he neared Abbotsford
his jaded spirits revived. When his home was
reached, dear friends surrounded him, his
favorite dogs rushed excitedly to welcome him
and rubbed their noses against his hands and
leaped up to kiss him. Then the strong man
broke down, he sobbed like a child and his
heart was filled with a strange joy.

He lingered for a little while. Each day
loving hands wheeled him around the beautiful grounds at Abbotsford. He admired the
roses, patted each dog fondly on the head and
gently stroked the hair of his grandchildren.
"I have seen much in my time," he said, "but
nothing like my ain house—give me one turn
more."

One day his son-in-law and biographer, J.
G. Lockhart, was sitting by his side. "Read
to me," said Scott. Lockhart glanced at the
thousands of books resting upon the shelves.
"From what book shall I read?" he asked.
"Need you ask?" answered Scott, "there is but
one book." Lockhart understood; he took
down the Bible and read from the Gospel by
John:

*"Let not your heart be troubled; ye believe
in God, believe also in me. In my Father's
house are many mansions; if it were not so,*

I would have told you. I go to prepare a place for you."

Scott was deeply touched. "That is a great comfort," he murmured, "a great comfort." A few days later he called Lockhart again, and said: "My dear, be a good man . . . be a good man. Nothing else will give you any comfort when you come to lie here."

Scott died peacefully on September 21, 1832. He had not succeeded in clearing the entire debt but he made a magnificent attempt although the effort shortened and saddened his life. He left behind him the memory of a man who was one of the most interesting writers of all time and also one of the most honorable men who ever lived.

CHAPTER III.

A HOMESICK BOY WHO INVENTED TELEGRAPHY.

SOME time during 1811 a twenty-year-old American youth went to England in order to study painting. The passage across the ocean in those days took much longer, and was more of an adventure, than it is to-day. The youth—whose name was Samuel Morse—was lonely and homesick. His first letter home contained these words: "I only wish you had this letter to relieve your minds from anxiety, for while I am writing I can imagine mother wishing that she could hear of my arrival and thinking of thousands of accidents which may have befallen me. I wish that in an instant I could communicate the information; but three thousand miles are not passed over in an instant, and we must wait at least four long weeks before we can hear from each other." It was this long wait of four or five weeks which distressed young Samuel Morse. He was anxious to hear from home and he knew that his father and mother would be very much worried until they received his letter.

He was born at Charlestown, Massachusetts on April 27, 1791. The first school he attended was kept by an old lady who was known as "Old Ma'am Rand." She governed her unruly flock with a long switch which almost reached across the small room where they were gathered. One of her forms of punishment was to pin the culprits to her dress. Almost from infancy Samuel Morse had shown ability to draw and one day when in school he drew a picture of "Old Ma'am Rand's" face and she saw it. Perhaps it was not a flattering picture as it certainly displeased the schoolmistress and by way of punishment she pinned Samuel to her dress; he squirmed and wriggled so much that the dress parted and he fled to the other side of the room. That afternoon "Ma'am Rand" gave her right hand considerable exercise and a certain young artist named Samuel Morse was the victim.

Samuel entered Yale College when he was only fourteen. At that time, which was long before the discovery of photography, portrait painting was a lucrative profession for those who had artistic ability and young Morse had quite made up his mind to become an artist. While at college he made many miniature pictures of his student friends and his skill astonished them. He also became greatly interested in the subject of electricity and in nearly every letter he wrote to his parents he mentioned the lectures of Professor Day. On March 8, 1809, he wrote to his mother: "Professor Day's lectures on electricity are very interesting and he has given some very fine experiments. To-day he made the whole class hold hands and form a circuit; then he gave us all a lively shock." But at that time there were no openings for a career in electricity and after graduation in 1810 Samuel Morse decided to visit England to improve his knowledge of art.

At that time there was in England, a famous American artist, Benjamin West, and young Morse carried letters of introduction to him. West received this young fellow-countryman and in addition to giving him lessons, he showed him many favors and put him in touch with such people as could help him. Morse's ability was soon recognized and in 1813 he won the gold medal of the Society of Arts for designing a figure representing the "Death of Hercules." A large painting which he also made on the same subject was admitted to the Royal Academy. One of the British newspapers ranked it among the nine best in a gallery of over a thousand paintings. This picture is now in the Art Museum of Yale University.

Morse returned to America in 1815, when he was twenty-four, and opened a studio in Boston. He did not meet with much success and for several years he earned a somewhat scant living. His work was generally praised but there was little demand for large paintings and he kept alive only by painting portraits for which he received five dollars each. He went to Washington and executed a large painting in which were likenesses of seventy Congress representatives; it was heartily praised by all but as no one cared to buy it Morse was worse off than ever. He had married in 1818 but he found it necessary to leave his wife in Boston and try to make a living in New York.

In August 1823 he wrote to tell his wife that he had found a place to board for two dollars and a quarter a week. In December of the same year he wrote to her: "My cash is almost gone and I am in great anxiety; I am completely at a loss to know what to do." He struggled along as best he could but when his wife died of heart disease in 1825, the blow, combined with the hardships he was facing, almost crushed him.

He had by no means lost his enthusiasm for electricity, indeed he watched the developments of the new science with great interest and whenever he heard of a lecture upon the subject he went if possible. He attended some experimental lectures by Professor James F. Dana which profoundly impressed him and turned his mind definitely toward the subject of electricity once more. In 1829 Morse sailed for Italy in order to paint some pictures for which he had received a commission. He remained there three years and in 1832—the most eventful year in Morse's life—he set sail for America.

On the voyage from Havre to New York several scientists were thrown together and electricity became the chief topic of discussion. A distinguished scientist, Dr. Charles F. Jackson, was asked if the velocity of electricity was in any way retarded by the length of the wire. Dr. Jackson replied that electricity passes instantaneously over any length of wire. This remark immediately fixed the attention of Samuel Morse. He said "I see no reason why intelligence may not be transmitted instantaneously by electricity." The conversation went on but the idea had completely taken possession of Samuel Morse. He could think of nothing else; he said the idea of instantaneous communication came to him with the full force of an electric shock. When he bade the Captain of the *Sully* good-bye at New York he said half in joke, half in earnest: "Do not be surprised if some day I discover the secret of instantaneous communication by electricity."

When Morse returned to New York in 1832 he found that his place as an artist had been filled, indeed he was almost forgotten, and for the next few years the struggle to live became harder than anything he had ever known. More than once he was practically reduced to starvation. He secured some pupils to whom he taught painting at a very low figure. His hopes were raised when it was decided to decorate the rotunda of the National Capitol in Washington. A number of artists were to be engaged and Morse felt sure that his work was such as to make an appointment sure. By some petty prejudice he was rejected and he felt the blow was both cruel and unjust.

Relief came at last in 1835 when he was appointed to a position in the Arts Department of New York University and here he worked at his calling by day and labored steadily with electrical experiments at night. Like all inventors he made many futile attempts to discover elusive secrets. He stretched coils of wire around his room and labored incessantly to send his code instantaneously over the stretch. He was desperately in need of financial aid and he was fortunate in getting Mr. Alfred Vail, a son of Judge Stephen Vail, interested. The two entered partnership and developments were soon forthcoming.

Morse had about seventeen hundred feet of wire stretched back and forth in the cabinet room of the University and on September 2, 1837, he made a successful experiment. The telegraph system worked. It was a success beyond the wildest dreams of Morse himself. He took an improved instrument to Washington and exhibited his invention on a ten mile circuit to President Van Buren and his cabinet, members of Congress, foreign ministers and men of science. A petition for a patent was filed at once.

The public, however, were far from convinced that the whole thing was not a gigantic hoax and that any money given to finance so weird and mysterious an invention would be lost. Morse's partners at this time suffered severe financial losses and they were no longer able to help him and Morse was compelled to go back to his portrait painting in order to make even a modest living. At this time the inventor received all manner of criticism but scarcely any encouragement and had he not been a man of strong will he would have given up in despair.

Toward the close of 1838 Morse determined to go to Washington and make an appeal for thirty thousand dollars so that he might construct telegraph communication between Washington and Baltimore and thus demonstrate that his invention was not a fraud as some insisted, nor a wild dream, but a marvellously useful thing. The long session of Congress dragged on and it appeared certain that his request would never be up for consideration.

The last day of the session arrived and there was a mass of accumulated business that required attention. Morse remained in the strangers' gallery until ten o'clock at night in an agony of suspense. Then weary and nearly heartbroken he left in despair where he spent a restless night. Next morning, as he came downstairs a young lady, Miss Ellsworth, whom he knew rushed up to him and said: "I want to congratulate you!" "What for?" said Morse with a puzzled look. "On the success of your bill; your request was granted." It was true, the bill had passed during the dying moments of the Congress.

With the help of Congress, Morse instantly began to work on the construction of a forty mile line between Washington and Baltimore. An attempt was first made to lay the wires underground but this had to be abandoned and the wires were eventually strung on poles above ground in the way familiar to everyone to-day. There were disappointments, mistakes and mishaps, but the line was completed in May 1844.

On that day, with the attention of hundreds of thousands upon him, Morse sat in a room of the Supreme Court at Washington and Miss Ellsworth handed him a slip of paper bearing the message she had chosen—"What hath God wrought." Within a minute it had been received at Baltimore by Alfred Vail, who at once signalled back the same four words. The dream of many years had been fulfilled; instantaneous communication by electricity was firmly established.

When Morse sought to introduce his marvellous invention to England he met with considerable opposition. With the exception of the railway companies few people regarded telegraphy with favor until a very curious happening made it popular. A brutal murder had been committed in London and it was known that the murderer had boarded a train for Paddington station in a distant part of the city. How could a message be sent swiftly to Paddington and the murderer's arrest brought about? The Great Western Railway had a

telegraph line and a description of the man
wanted was flashed over the wires, and when
he arrived at the station the police were waiting for him. This dramatic arrest caught the
popular fancy and completely broke down the
foolish prejudice against telegraphy.

After years of discouragement Samuel
Morse lived to enjoy the fruits of his labors.
Honors came to him from almost every country and he was elected to membership in
learned societies in a score of countries. His
biographer says: "A greater number of honorary distinctions were bestowed upon him
than were ever given to any other private citizen." A magnificent bronze statue of Morse
was erected in Central Park, New York, and
was unveiled amid scenes of great enthusiasm
on June 10, 1871.

Samuel Morse lived to be almost eighty-
one; he died on April 1, 1872. Long after
he discovered telegraphy he came across the
letter he had written when homesick in 1810,
in which he had longed for "instant communication" with his parents in far-off America.
The old inventor took the envelope, yellow
with age, and wrote across it: "I was longing
for a telegraph even when I wrote this letter."
Thus it was that the homesickness of a lonely
youth was partly responsible for one of the
most useful inventions of all time.

CHAPTER IV.

He Turned the World's Ridicule Into Cheers.

A T the beginning of last century, long before moving pictures had ever been thought of, an ingenious American named Robert Fulton was living in Paris, France, and trying hard to interest others in his invention. Not long previous, the City of Moscow had been destroyed by fire, so he engaged a large building and erected an immense canvas which portrayed the burning of Moscow. Thousands came to see it, many from great distances, and Robert Fulton made enough money from the admission fees to keep himself while he worked away at his inventions. The street where this was shown was the "rue des Panorames," and Fulton's invention was called a "Panorama." For nearly a hundred years panoramas were very popular everywhere, but Fulton's was the first of them all.

Robert Fulton was born at Little Britain, Pennsylvania, U.S.A., on November 14, 1765. His father died when Robert was three years old and, as there were five little children all under eight, the struggle to make both ends meet was severe for his widowed mother. From earliest boyhood Robert was of an inventive turn of mind; he seemed restless unless he was trying to invent something.

When he was fourteen he had a friend named Christopher Gumpf. This boy's father was fond of fishing and he used to take the two boys with him so that they might row the boat from place to place in the creek during the fishing. Robert's arms ached and he told his chum that he became very tired with so much rowing. Soon his brain was busy and he invented a set of paddles to work at the side of the boat to be operated by a double crank. Two pieces of lumber were fastened together at right angles with a wide paddle at each end. The crank was attached to the boat near the stern, with the paddle operating on a pivot as a rudder. The next time the old gentleman went fishing and took the boys with him, he saw Robert's invention, and was delighted with it. After that the fishing trips were days of fun for the boys.

Robert Fulton wanted to become an artist and when he was seventeen he went to Philadelphia where he set up business as a portrait painter. He was quite gifted at this work and did so well that he made enough money to return home at the end of three years and buy a small farm for his mother, and to help in the education of his brothers and sisters.

When he was twenty-two Robert went to England with letters of introduction to Benjamin West, another Pennsylvania youth who had established a fine reputation as a painter. West took a great interest in the boy from his own state and through him Robert Fulton met many distinguished people. Some of these men were great engineers; gradually his love of inventing came back to him and he decided to devote his life to scientific engineering. He became greatly interested in canals. At that time the roads of England were bad; in the United States they were much worse, and as the railway train had not yet been invented Fulton believed that most of the commerce would be carried on by systems of water canals in each country. During these years Fulton remained very poor. He had arrived in England with only two hundred and fifty dollars, and this was soon spent. Often he was so reduced in circumstances that he was compelled to borrow from his friends. On one occasion he had less than sixty cents, yet all the while he was thinking great thoughts and planning things which were destined to alter the history of the human race.

After ten years in England, Fulton went to France and it was during this period that he invented the Panorama. His inventive mind was more active than ever. He invented an undersea armored boat which could be submerged at will, and be brought to the surface again. This was the beginning of the torpedo boat which later became so much used in naval warfare. It seems strange now, but Robert Fulton believed that the invention of submarines would abolish naval warfare, for already he had recognized that war was a great evil.

In 1800 Fulton completed the first submarine, which he named the *Nautilus*. Of course, his invention was greeted with a good deal of ridicule. Many called him a fool and some of his friends even felt that the invention was little more than a wild dream. In order to show his faith in the submarine, Fulton remained on board with three other men while the trial was made. The *Nautilus* was submerged to a depth of twenty-five feet in the River Seine, and there, with only two candles for light, the men remained for one hour and then safely came to the surface. Later, Fulton went with the boat to Havre where he again went below the surface with it, and even made several journeys under water.

Napoleon Bonaparte became interested in the invention. He sent for Fulton and listened while the American inventor explained the possibilities of the submarine. Nothing came of the interview. Napoleon, whose mind was fixed on warfare and who hesitated at nothing which would further his ends, became convinced that the invention was little more than a brilliant toy, and Fulton was dismissed. In 1803 Fulton returned to England where he remained three years, but while the British Government showed considerable interest in his inventions, they did not come to any satisfactory understanding with Fulton. The British Government, however, treated him generously and gave him over seventy thousand dollars so that for the first time in his life Fulton was able to devote himself entirely to invention without being worried about money matters.

Fulton returned to America in 1806 and at once began to lay plans for building a commercial steamboat service on the River Hudson. While in France he had formed a friendship with Mr. Robert L. Livingston, the Ambassador to that country. These two men became business partners and Fulton built the *Clermont* which he proposed should sail on the Hudson River under its own steam, something which had never yet been attempted in America. Three years before, Fulton had operated his boat on the Seine, and while onlookers laughed and ridiculed him he went ahead with the construction of the *Clermont*. The boat was one hundred and thirty-three feet long, eighteen feet wide and its tonnage was one hundred and sixty.

At this time Fulton was exposed to both opposition and ridicule. He was nicknamed "Toot" Fulton because of the noise made by the Watt engine which he had imported from England. Thousands came to see the *Clermont,* and by many she was named "Fulton's Folly." He needed more money to complete the vessel, but his friends who loaned him what he needed, did so on condition that their names should not be made known as they did not want to be laughed at for backing a wild scheme.

On the morning of August 10, 1806, the banks of the Hudson River were lined with thousands of spectators who came to see the triumph or the humiliation of Robert Fulton. Crowds assembled on the wharves, piers, and even on the house-tops near the river. That any kind of vessel should be propelled through the waters except by oars or sails, seemed unbelievable to most of these onlookers, but they had sufficient curiosity to witness the experiment. Among the interested spectators was Miss Helen Livingston who later became Fulton's wife.

Slowly and clumsily the *Clermont* left her moorings with forty people on board, and Fulton in command. Thousands of spectators gazed with suppressed excitement as the engine spluttered and hissed. Would the vessel go? Both wind and tide were against her; would she be carried down the river with the tide? The *Clermont* began to move; slowly but steadily until all could see that she was making headway against tide and wind. Cheers arose, faint at first, then louder and clearer, until they were deafening; jeers were turned into cheers. Then engine was being fed with pine logs and black smoke belched from her chimney. Keeping a speed of more than five miles an hour against the tide, the *Clermont* steamed to Albany, a distance of one hundred and fifty miles.

Fulton rapidly made great improvements and during the next nine years he built fifteen steamboats. Soon there was a regular steamboat service between New York and Albany. At first boats ran at long intervals; others were added and three trips a week were made, the fare being seven dollars each way. Then regular stopping places were established, and short distances could be covered, the minimum fare being one dollar. In 1816 Fulton built the *Chancellor Livingston* with a tonnage of five hundred and twenty-six, and having first and second-class cabins, double tiers of sleeping berths, kitchens and many other conveniences. An invention had come which was destined to change ocean travel the world over.

Fulton also invented the first steam ferry boat. The vessel had two rounded ends with paddles between them, and carried horses and carriages, as well as passengers, between New York and Jersey City. Even as early as 1811 these ferry boats were giving a half-hour service, and as the only service had been by row boat, the new enterprise proved a great boon to the people. Of course, all Fulton's steamboats burned wood; the boiler stood above deck, and the paddle wheels were not enclosed. There was danger of the wheels becoming entangled with ropes, and of the passengers getting splashed, so the wheels were covered.

It is a remarkable thing that this man who had such a poor education when a boy; who was almost altogether self-taught, should have achieved so much for the benefit of his fellows. He was a hard worker. When he was in

France he learned the French, Italian and German languages, in addition to mathematics, physics and chemistry. He had restless energy, and fully believed that his inventions would greatly increase human happiness. He died on February 23, 1815, before he had reached his fiftieth birthday, and was buried in the graveyard of Trinity Church, New York, which now nestles amidst the towering skyscrapers of that great city.

CHAPTER V.

THE GRANDSON OF A SLAVE WHOSE SINGING REACHES ALL HEARTS.

IN 1887 a negro boy was born in a little cabin in Curryville, Georgia. His grandfather had been a slave, and after the Civil War, when several hundred acres had been given out to former slaves, he secured a ten-acre allotment. When Roland Hayes—for that was the name of the negro boy—was born, his father was struggling hard to provide for his growing family but he was injured by a falling log and crushed so severely that his spine was never right again; for the remainder of his life he was a cripple. The mother of Roland Hayes and the children, all of whom were quite young, had to carry on the work of the small farm. This they did so well that they were able to rent an additional piece of land on which they raised more produce, half of which they kept and half went to the owner.

Curryville was several miles from any railway and was so small that it could not be called a village. Here in a community where the neighbors were all as poor, if not poorer

than the Hayes family, Roland Hayes grew
up and as a small boy learned to do a man's
work and do it cheerfully. Sometimes there
was a teacher at the tiny school; but more than
half the time it was closed with the result that
when Roland was a big boy he could read and
write only with difficulty. His mother was
without money and quite without education
but she had a tender heart and great understanding so she resolved to sell all she had and
move to Chattanooga, Tennessee, where her
children would have a better chance. When
Roland was fifteen his mother sold their crop
for that year, also their cow and horse, and the
family said farewell to the tiny cabin which
had been their home.

Roland found work in a factory where
weights for window frames were manufactured. It was the hardest work the boy had
ever tackled. He had to carry ladles brim-
ming with melted iron and pour it into cast-
ings where it was left to cool and harden.
The scars and bruises the boy received when
at that job have remained with him for thirty
years, but as he received eighty cents a day
he bore the long hours and hard work without
a murmur. After a while his salary was raised
to a dollar a day and so he remained in that
factory for a year, until it was his turn to go

to school as he and his brothers attended school in turn.

When the school term was over Roland went back to the factory and was soon put in charge of the core department at a salary of three dollars a day, so he decided not to return to school but to take lessons from a teacher in the evenings. Life in Chattanooga was different from Curryville and much more interesting. He joined the choir of a little colored church and when he took his place among the singers there was no prouder boy in the city. In those days he had no thought of ever becoming a great singer, he sang because he loved it; sometimes when singing he closed his eyes and it was easy for his listeners to know that he sang from his heart.

Roland sang as he went about his work in the factory. One day when he was singing the foreman raised his hand for others to cease so that the clear sweet voice of the young negro might be heard by all. Although Roland Hayes did not notice it himself, when he began to sing, all whistling and talking would cease and his work-mates eagerly listened.

When Roland was seventeen a young negro named Arthur Calhoun, a student at Oberlin University who was taking a year off in order to make some money, heard him sing and a warm friendship sprang up between the two. Calhoun, although a singer himself, went into raptures over Roland's rich tenor voice and tried to convince him that he ought to devote himself to a musical career. Roland himself was not much taken with the idea and his mother was much opposed to it. She had great hopes for her boy but the thought of his being a singer had never once entered her mind. "Whoever heard of a colored man making a living by singing?" she asked. "No," she said, she wanted Roland to do something useful instead of wasting his time.

Arthur Calhoun was not one to be lightly turned aside when once he had made up his mind. He made an appointment with a white gentleman in Chattanooga so that this man might hear Roland sing. That visit was one of the never-to-be-forgotten events in Roland's life. When he and his friend arrived at the gentleman's home he was engaged and the negro boys waited in the hall. When at last they entered the room the man's wife and daughters quietly left—but not for long. When Roland began to sing they returned and listened with keen appreciation. Then the man put on some phonograph records by Caruso and many other great singers, and it was

Roland's turn to show open-mouthed admiration.

Everything seemed wonderful to the boy that night, the home, the furnishings, and this marvellous singing by great artists. He had never heard anything like it. Tears filled his eyes and when he and his friend left he could scarcely speak, and walked home as if in a dream. He scarcely spoke a word but when the time came to say good-bye to his friend, he said, with tears in his voice as well as his eyes: "I am going to study music."

The road to a musical education was not an easy one for Roland Hayes. First, his mother's objections had to be overcome but, although she was still unconvinced that it was a wise course, she gave her consent. He set out for Oberlin with fifty dollars. He decided to give concerts in small churches and thus pay his way, but the plan did not work very well. He was quite unknown; the admission fee he charged at his concerts was ten cents but it took a good many dimes to pay even for the cost of renting the buildings. Roland's fifty dollars dwindled until all he had left was five dollars. Then he was forced to seek admission to Fisk University which was much nearer than Oberlin. That night in the attic where he was staying, Roland earnestly prayed that God would open a way for him to attend college.

Next morning he called upon Dr. A. G. Merrill, President of Fisk University. Dr. Merrill listened to the boy's story and then said very kindly: "I am very sorry but all the openings for students who work their way through college are filled." It seemed to Roland that a door was being closed in his face. With tears streaming down his cheeks he pleaded for a chance—he would work at anything and he would never let anyone down who gave him encouragement. The President was touched and he made arrangements to have Roland stay with a family who lived some distance from the college. He was to be a general handy man around the home and in return would have his food, lodging, and one dollar a week. He was on trial for one month and if he succeeded in making a good record at Fisk, the arrangement would continue. At the end of the month Roland heard nothing and was afraid to ask any questions but he remained for a whole year.

When the year was up the President congratulated him both on his standing in college and on his work with the family whom he had been serving. During the second year he was given a position with a family in the college grounds which suited him much better. He remained at Fisk University for four years and caught up to the other students in class work although the little schooling he had when a boy was a terrible handicap.

After leaving Fisk he secured a position at the Pendennis Club at Louisville, Kentucky. One evening the manager asked him to sing at a big dinner party. His singing so thrilled the guests that they dispensed with the rest of the programme and called for Roland Hayes again and again. It was a great triumph for him. After that he sang frequently and was generally paid at the rate of five dollars for an evening. The President of Fisk University asked him to accompany some singers to Boston where a number of concerts were to be given. He offered him seventy-five dollars and his expenses. Hayes eagerly accepted the offer and felt that the tide against which he had been battling all his life had suddenly begun to turn in his favor.

While in Boston he decided to take vocal lessons from Mr. Arthur Hubbard, an outstanding music teacher who had shown a kindly interest in him. This meant that he had to earn every dollar he could in order to support himself and pay for his lessons. For a while he worked as a bell-boy in the Brunswick Hotel and later as a messenger boy for an insurance company for which he received seven dollars a week.

All his brothers and sisters had left home by now. He decided to take his mother to Boston and establish a humble home of their own. He went to Chattanooga and helped his mother to sell what few possessions she did not need. Then he took her to Boston where they rented a flat for four dollars and fifty cents a week. There was less than three dollars left for other expenses but by taking care of every cent the two got along. He made a bed for his mother out of the old box which had carried her belongings to Boston; he made tables, chairs, a bureau and his own bed out of other boxes. He was not a carpenter and some of the furniture did not look elegant, but it served his purpose and his mother, at least, was very proud of it.

For eight years Roland Hayes lived in this way all the while studying music and every day becoming a little surer of the wonderful gift that God had given him. He sang in churches and as more engagements came he was able to take good care of his mother and to put some money in the bank; money which he knew he would need when the time came for him to give recitals.

His first concerts were not a financial success but after some difficulty he engaged the famous Symphony Hall for a recital although nearly all his friends advised him against doing so. He had purchased a second-hand typewriter and he typed and sent out two thousand letters. When the evening for the concert came the great hall was packed to the doors and hundreds were turned away. His rich tenor voice, so full of passionate and tender feeling thrilled the vast audience and from that night his fame as a singer was made in one great city, at least.

A man who heard him sing asked him to go to Santa Monica in California and here again he repeated his great triumph in Boston. A man in Santa Monica said to him: "I have heard all the famous singers but there is something in your singing which is different from all the others; what is it?" Roland Hayes himself did not know what it was but he was much encouraged by what the man said and that night he lay in bed thinking over the man's words. Invitations to sing now poured in upon him from every direction and wherever he went it was the same; vast delighted audiences and praise such as would gladden any man's heart.

In 1920 Roland Hayes went to England

where by special invitation he sang for the King George V. and Queen Mary at Buckingham Palace.   Later he visited France, Germany, Austria and many other countries and wherever he sang, his marvellous voice and his modest, graceful bearing made a fine impression.   He has sung his way into people's hearts wherever he has gone, and it is not too much to say that to-day he is one of the world's most popular singers.

Roland Hayes remains one of the most modest men that ever lived; no praise seems to spoil him.   All his life he has believed that he is in the hands of God and that his career is being planned for him.   Many years ago, when living in the humble cabin in Georgia, his gentle and hard-working mother taught him that simple faith and it helped him during the years of hard struggle.   Perhaps it is this faith which enables him to reach people's hearts as, above everything else, this is the thing that Roland Hayes does and the world is better because he can do it.

CHAPTER VI.

A LONELY MAN WHOM BOYS WILL NEVER FORGET.

ON the morning of September 5, 1819, a fourteen-year-old boy named Hans Andersen arrived in Copenhagen. He came from Odense a small town on the island of Fiinen in Denmark. His father was a poor cobbler who, although he had no education himself, was anxious that Hans should learn to read and write. In those days there were no public schools and the fees at private schools were more than the cobbler could afford but he managed to get his boy into the "poor school" of the town.

The Andersens were poor—so poor that they lived in one mean room where there was little besides the shoemaker's bench, the rough bedstead, and a few homemade chairs. The father was a disappointed man; his greatest ambition in life had been to secure an education but his father had thought this was a very foolish idea and as a result the shoemaker, although an intelligent man, could neither read nor write. Many years afterward Hans

described the home of his boyhood. He wrote:
"Our little room was almost filled with the
shoemaker's bench, the bed and my crib. The
walls were covered with pictures and over the
work bench was a cupboard containing books
and songs; the little kitchen was full of shin-
ing plates and metal pans, and by means of a
ladder it was possible to go out on the roof
where, in the gutters between it and the neighbor's house, there was a great chest filled with
soil. This was my dear mother's garden,
where she grew her vegetables . . . my
mother always kept our room clean and neat
and took great pride in having the bed linen
and the curtains very white."

Hans Andersen was a strange child. He
made a toy theater and spent every spare moment he had, manipulating the tiny dolls and
reading aloud the plays of Shakespeare while
he pretended that the dolls were playing the
parts. He had such a wonderful imagination
that he could completely ignore his miserable
surroundings; he forgot the dingy room and
his threadbare and patched clothes. He was
as happy as a king, clothed in purple and living in a beautiful castle. When Hans was
eleven years old his father died, and the
family was in worse circumstances than before.

Hans was not a promising pupil at school and his head seemed full of strange fancies. He was constantly making up stories and telling them to children. He went to work in a cloth factory but he disliked both the work and the rough work-mates who constantly teased the lad and played rough jokes upon him so that he really became afraid of them, and his mother took him away from the place. He wrote little plays and stories but as the spelling and grammar were all wrong no one paid any attention to what he wrote. Then something happened which excited Hans very much and changed his whole life.

Some strolling players from Copenhagen visited Odense; as it was a small out-of-the-way place this visit created a great deal of interest. For some scenes in their plays the actors needed "supers" and a number of Odense people were engaged. Great was the astonishment and amusement of the audience when the ungainly looking boy, Hans Andersen, appeared among these local "supers." He was tall, painfully thin, and had big wide-staring eyes, which always made him look as if he had been suddenly startled; also he had a very large nose and enormous feet for a boy. But the washerwoman's son, who had played with his dolls and toy theater all his life, could not resist the temptation to appear on the stage when he got a chance. Of course, Hans was teased and made fun of more than ever, but shy and sensitive though he was he never forgot the thrill of appearing before the public.

When he was fourteen Hans begged his mother's permission to go to Copenhagen. "What will a poor boy like you do in Copenhagen?" his mother asked. "I will be famous," replied Hans, "people have much hardship to go through at first; then afterwards they become famous." His mother despaired of changing his mind and so, giving him the seven dollars he had saved, she allowed him to go to the great city. Arrayed in his best clothes, and wearing his father's overcoat Hans made his way to Copenhagen.

He first called upon a Madam Schall who taught dancing. His tall lean form and awkward appearance almost frightened her. When he told her that he wished to be an actor, she asked: "What can you do?" "I can play Cinderella," he said, "I have seen it performed at Odense." He drew off his boots and using his hat as a tambourine began to dance and sing. His wild appearance and wide-staring eyes made her think that the lad was demented and she was very glad to get him out of the house.

He had told his mother when he left that he was prepared for hardship and was not afraid. He needed all his courage. Penniless and alone in a great city he was soon reduced to starvation. He tried to get work by singing or reciting at the theaters but he was turned roughly away. He worked one day in a carpenter's shop but he could not stand the rough jokes and ridicule of the men. He prayed earnestly that God would help him and one morning he decided to go to the Academy of Music and seek an interview with the director.

The director was a famous Italian named Siboni and on the evening that Hans Andersen called he was giving a large dinner-party. Siboni and his guests decided to hear him sing and recite. The unhappy boy did his best but suddenly he seemed to remember his unhappy condition and he burst into tears. Siboni and his guests felt sorry for the boy and showed him considerable kindness. The director took up a subscription for him and made arrangements to have his voice trained. Hans' prospects looked brighter; he was received into the home of a professor of vocal music and learned a good deal about singing. But the result of his poverty had told upon his health. He had trudged through the streets with bad shoes in winter and had never worn sufficient warm clothing. As a result his voice lost its sweetness, then broke, and Siboni advised him to return to Odense and learn some useful trade.

Hans then wrote to a poet in Copenhagen named Guldberg to whom he stated his cir-circumstances. This man proved a friend indeed. He saw that the boy was lacking in education and he himself gave him lessons in the Danish language and got others to teach him other subjects. Through Guldberg, Hans made the acquaintance of a Mr. Jonas Collin who managed to interest King Frederick VI in the boy. The King made him an allowance on condition that Hans would return to school and improve his education which was sadly deficient.

Hans went back to school although he was not fond of study. There were some subjects he did not seem to understand at all and he was constantly writing poetry and making up fanciful stories. The master of the school was a stern man who took a dislike to poor Hans. More than once this man came across pieces of poetry that the boy had written and he delighted in reading them aloud in class and holding Hans up to ridicule.

During the holidays Hans and some others

were invited to the home of a distinguished man in Copenhagen where a number of musicians and poets gathered. Hans had never before been in so beautiful a home, with such brilliant lights and marvellous pictures. The boy, however, was not altogether happy there as he suddenly realized that he was by far the shabbiest dressed person in the room and he tried to hide behind the long curtains. A poet came to Hans and shook his hand kindly, and the boy was so overcome with gratitude that he could scarcely speak. Of these days Hans wrote later: "I endured much bitter want but I told it to none, else many would have helped me to the utmost of their means. A false shame prevented me from confessing what I endured."

Hans Andersen began to publish some books of poetry and stories. At first his books were much criticized. His writing was so different from that of other authors. The strange fancies which had filled his mind when a boy were more active than ever. To his lively imagination there was nothing dead in all the world; everything was alive and talked. In his stories there were conversations between flowers and animals; remarks wise and otherwise came from darning-needles, shadows, shillings, fir-trees, ducklings and old street lamps. No wonder some people were bewildered.

But his books were marvellous and even those who scoffed at him were compelled to admit it. In 1831 his health completely broke down, chiefly owing to the severe hardships of his life, but two years later he was granted a small pension by the government and this relieved his mind of a great deal of worry. In 1835 he published a book of fairy tales which are known the whole world over. Some of his tales are: "The Steadfast Tin Soldier," "The Ugly Duckling," "The Storks," "The Flying Trunk" and "The Goloshes of Fortune." Many of these fairy tales are among the most charming ever written.

In 1840 he wrote a book entitled: "Picture Book Without Pictures" which created quite a sensation. Many years before, when he was a poor, shabbily-dressed boy in Odense people had laughed when they saw him surrounded by children to whom he told stories. Sometimes the tales were funny; at other times sad, but they were always interesting. Now that he had become a man, once more Hans Andersen turned to the children and before long the boys and girls, not only in Denmark, but in a score of different countries laughed and cried over his delightful fairy tales. Probably none of them knew how much of hardship and loneliness the gentle author of these tales had known.

Hans Andersen was given a pension by the King and he began to travel through many countries and wherever he went this big, awkward, tender-hearted man was a great favorite. When in England he was the guest of Charles Dickens and these two men—both lovers of children—greatly admired each other. Dickens went to the pier to bid Hans Andersen good-bye when he left England. The next book that Andersen wrote he dedicated to Charles Dickens. Hans also met Sir Walter Scott, Mrs. Robert Browning and many other notable persons.

Hans Andersen wrote many stories which eventually made him a famous man. His books, published in English, fill ten large volumes and in 1900 an edition of his "Tales" appeared in six different languages. His own countrymen conferred upon him the Grand Cross of the Dannebrog Order and now there is no name more honored in Denmark than that of the obscure son of a cobbler. Odense, which once had treated him shabbily, now hastened to make amends. In 1867 he was made an honorary citizen of his native town and to-day there is a magnificent monument erected there to his memory.

King Christian VIII of Denmark and his queen were very fond of the story-teller and he was frequently invited to be their guest at the royal table. On such occasions he was always asked to read some tales from his books and he became greatly honored as he well deserved to be, for he was a man with nothing but kindness and gentleness in his heart. He died at Copenhagen on August 4, 1875. He was Denmark's great gift to the world.

CHAPTER VII.

HIS DIFFICULTIES PAVED THE WAY TO SUCCESS.

A LITTLE over a century ago an English boy named Isaac Pitman was attending a school at Trowbridge, in Wiltshire. The building was very small—twenty-five feet by fifteen—and as there were about one hundred boys in attendance the air often became heavy as the scholars droned over their lessons. Perhaps that was the reason that young Isaac Pitman became subject to fainting fits and often had to be carried out of the school into the fresh air. These fits became so frequent that the boy's parents decided to take him away from school, so in October, 1825, when he was in his thirteenth year, Isaac Pitman said good-bye to his schoolmates.

Soon afterwards he began to work in the office of a clothing factory where the hours were from six in the morning until six in the evening. The novelty of being free from school soon wore off, and besides, he regretted the fact that he had so little education and pleaded with his father for permission to return to school. His request was refused but he resolved to study at home, and in order to do this he got up mornings at four and spent two hours over his lessons before going to work. In addition to this, he studied again in the evening before going to bed. There was a lending library in the town and Isaac made good use of it. By the time he was sixteen he had read many of the best books in the library and had committed to memory long passages from the Bible, which he could recite without hesitation.

Although Isaac was a great reader, he met very few educated people and he soon discovered that he mispronounced many familiar words. He knew what the words meant, but they were seldom used in any conversations he heard. He determined to remedy this and bought *Walker's Dictionary*. He read the book through from cover to cover and made a list of all the words which he was in the habit of mispronouncing. He found there were over two thousand words on his list, and all had to be gone over carefully until he had the correct pronunciation.

When Isaac was eighteen, he decided to become a school teacher. He went to a training school for teachers and in five months he was ready to take his first appointment. The years he had spent in careful study stood him in good stead, and he was an apt pupil. His first school was at Barton and his salary was fixed at a little over six dollars a week. As he was one of eleven children, his parents were not able to help him very much and when he reached Barton he had less than two dollars in the world.

He was an excellent schoolmaster and was greatly beloved by the people of the village, as well as by the pupils in school. The fact that he left school himself soon after his twelfth birthday made him a more sympathetic teacher. He understood better than did his pupils what a handicap it is to face the world without a good education, and he was never too busy to help his boys. He was much interested in correct pronunciation and regretted the fact that so many words were not pronounced as their spelling would suggest. He was greatly in favor of a system of simplified spelling.

A cousin loaned him a book about shorthand written by Samuel Taylor. It was a large book, expensive and not very satisfactory; however, Isaac Pitman was interested in it and tried hard to make it clear to his boys. He decided to publish a little manual explaining the system, which could be sold for six cents a copy. A newspaper reporter suggested to him that, instead of trying to explain Taylor's difficult system, he should invent a system of his own; one that would be so simple and easily understood that it could be explained by a small pamphlet instead of an expensive book with several hundred pages.

Up to that time Isaac Pitman had never thought about such a thing, but once the suggestion was made the idea took root and he could think of nothing else. He resolved to make his system absolutely different from any that had preceded it. It would be *Phonetic,* built upon the sounds of words, and he immediately began to plan for it. He was at this time twenty-four years of age and he worked at his *Phonetic System of Shorthand* in every spare moment he had.

The first edition of the little manual of Shorthand by Isaac Pitman was published in November, 1837. It was so much simpler and better in every way than any previous attempts at inventing a system that it immediately became popular although, strange to say, there was a considerable amount of opposition. Articles appeared in several newspapers and magazines, either approving or ridiculing the system, but Pitman undertook to go on a lecture tour and in Manchester, Glasgow and many other cities, he completely silenced his critics and proved the great value of his shorthand system.

At this time the cost of sending letters was very high. To send a single sheet of paper in an envelope cost nineteen cents, while for larger letters, especially when sent long distances, the cost was so great that only well-to-do people could send letters by mail. When the *Penny Post* was established and it became possible to send letters all over the country for two cents, it was hailed as a great boon by the people. Isaac Pitman soon saw the advantages of *Penny Postage* and he offered to teach his system by mail to any who would apply for lessons. Soon he had hundreds— if not thousands—studying shorthand in all parts of the country and the knowledge of his marvellous system spread everywhere.

It is not easy to tell what the coming of shorthand meant to the people of one hundred years ago. Soon speeches, sermons, reports of meetings and general news were reported quickly and accurately, and the improvement in newspapers and magazines was remarkable. At first many absolutely refused to believe that a reporter could take down a speech as it was being delivered, but soon even rapid speakers could be easily reported by following

Pitman's marvellous system. Pitman has been instrumental in giving millions of speeches to the reading public.

Pitman removed to Bath where he opened a school for the study of shorthand. Soon schools were begun in other places until there was a network of such schools all over Great Britain. In Great Britain the system is now practised everywhere; in the United States it is in general use. It is used in Africa wherever civilization has penetrated; in India the system is understood from Colombo to the Himalayas; in China and Japan it is equally well-known. It has been adapted to a score of languages other than English. Few inventions of the Nineteenth Century—or any other century for that matter—have done more to bring knowledge into the homes of common people.

In 1894 he was knighted by Queen Victoria in recognition of his great services to humanity, and this honor met with general approval. The life of Sir Isaac Pitman is a striking illustration of how a man may overcome great obstacles and make them

Stepping-stones to higher things.

He was always handicapped by poor health, and further, by the fact that because of this poor health, he had to leave school when little over twelve years of age and work from twelve to thirteen hours a day during those years when most boys, fortunately, are having a good time.

Soon after he was twenty-four Isaac Pitman resolved to become a total abstainer from alcohol. Previous to that time he had, like many men of his time, kept a barrel of beer in his home. One day he knocked the bung out of this barrel and poured its contents into the sewer, and for the remainder of his life he never used intoxicating liquor in any form. He was also a vegetarian and a non-smoker. He lived to be eighty-four years of age, and almost until the closing months of his life he was seated at his office desk, ready for business, at six o'clock each morning.

His useful life came to a close on Friday, January 22, 1897. To his pastor, who was with him to the end, he gave this message: "To those who ask how Isaac Pitman passed away, say, 'peacefully, and with no more concern than in passing from one room into another.'" His funeral at Bath was attended by the Mayor and by a vast number of citizens. Tributes to his kind and gracious character, as well as to his great service to humanity, came from all over the world. Mr.

T. M. Healy, a distinguished parliamentarian of his day, said: "Isaac Pitman was one of the finest and greatest men of the Nineteenth Century."

CHAPTER VIII.

HE COULD STAND ANYTHING EXCEPT PITY.

DURING the American Civil War there was so much coming and going of soldiers in some towns that it is no wonder boys became excited by what they saw and heard. Mimic battles and parades became the rage and whenever a boy could lay his hand on a gun he wanted to play with it. In one case at least this led to serious consequences.

In 1864 there was a boy living in Kalamazoo, Michigan, named Robert H. Babcock, who had learned to use a gun. One day his eight-year-old brother made a toy pistol out of a hollow key he found. He bored a hole near the base of the handle and fixed in it something that looked like a trigger. He showed it to his brother Robert and the two procured some powder and went to their father's barn where they tried to shoot with it. For some reason it would not work and so, not to be cheated out of their fun, they tried to make a bomb of some powder and a live coal. They set in with a slow torch and retired to the other end of the barn and waited; nothing happened. Then Robert went to investigate and when his face was quite near the bomb it exploded; he was instantly blinded and remained so for the rest of his life.

As soon as his parents realized that there was absolutely no hope of his sight being restored they took Robert to an institute for the blind in Philadelphia where he remained for three years. There could not have been a lonelier boy in the world than Robert Babcock that first night he spent in the institute. Perhaps he did not know it at the time but when his parents kissed him good-bye that night they felt as badly if not worse than he did. They realized, however, that if Robert stayed at home he would probably become pitied and pampered so much that it would spoil him. They wanted him to develop self-reliance and to learn how to look after himself; never did a boy receive a lesson in better spirit.

Robert took his place among the scores of other blind boys in the Philadelphia institution. Just a short time before he had been running around Kalamazoo, as lively and merry-hearted a boy as there was in the town; now totally blind he groped his way around corridors and learned to read the raised

Braille type as other blind people did. One thing his mother had done out of the kindness of her heart caused him some worry. She bought him a wash-stand which was to be for his use alone. That wash-stand was a nuisance. The other boys teased him about it from the beginning and Robert had it taken away. He decided to face his trouble as other lads faced theirs and refused to be treated differently.

From the beginning of his trouble Robert Babcock proved a hero. He was sensitive about his blindness and that which hurt him more than anything else was to have others pity him. Well-meaning people often spoke to him in such tones that, although they did not know it, every word they uttered cut him like a whip. "Why can't they forget I am blind?" he said, "and treat me as an ordinary person?"

He got along so well at the Institute that when the first Christmas came he decided to travel alone, the long distance from Philadelphia to Kalamazoo. There were several changes to be made at railway stations and some of his friends tried to persuade him against travelling alone. But Robert wanted to develop self-reliance and learn how to get about himself. "I have a tongue," he said, "and I am not afraid to ask questions."

At Pittsburgh station a man, noticing that he was blind, approached him and asked abruptly, "How did you become blind?" The sensitive lad hesitated then said: "By the explosion of a bombshell." "Oh I see!" the man went on, "you were a drummer in the war." The conclusion was flattering and Robert, who did not want to continue the conversation, said nothing but moved away.

Between Pittsburgh and Cleveland the train ran into a heavy snowstorm which delayed it for several hours. One of Robert's cousins was to have met him at Cleveland but he got tired of waiting and went home. So it was that, at two o'clock in the morning, Robert Babcock arrived at the station after having been in a day-coach for nearly thirty hours. It looked as if he would have to spend the remainder of that winter night in the cold station but the big-hearted train conductor saw him. "Come along with me," he said, "I've got an extra bed at home and you can sleep there." The cousin was located the following day and the two went from Cleveland to Kalamazoo.

After three years Robert went from Philadelphia to Olivet to prepare for college. Olivet school was different in many ways from the Institute he had left. He was the only blind boy there and to take his place in the various classes side by side with boys who could see was certainly a great test. At Olivet Robert proved himself to be a good student and one of the best-natured boys in the school. He attended lectures and his roommate read to him from the class textbooks. Like most blind people he developed a fine memory and remarkable power of concentration. Each year his standing in class was near the top; he won the admiration alike of students and teachers.

In 1869—when he was eighteen—Robert entered Western Reserve College and later began to study at Ann Arbor Medical College. It is believed that he was the first student to begin the study of medicine after a complete loss of sight. From Ann Arbor he went to study at the Chicago Medical School. Part of his examination in Chicago was the task of dissecting a body, something which even students with good eyesight find difficult. Sightless though he was, Robert managed to pass this test to the great satisfaction and astonishment of the examining board. From Chicago he went to study for a while at the College of Physicians and Surgeons in New York City where his record was exceptionally brilliant. After studying medicine for nine years he began to practice in Chicago.

His father offered to assist him financially until he was well-established. Again Robert's spirit of self-reliance asserted itself and he determined to pay his own way. It took him ten years to build up a strong practice. During this period he worked very hard, frequently crossing from one end of the city to another in order to make visits which often brought him only two dollars each.

After some years Babcock's exceptional ability was generally recognized. He frequently addressed the physicians of the city and eventually was appointed a Professor of the Chicago College of Physicians and Surgeons and was also made an Attending Physician of Cook County Hospital. Later he was made Professor of Diseases of the Chest and Clinical Medicine. He bought a typewriter and soon became an expert in using it. During these years Doctor Babcock wrote three important medical books which did much to make him a world figure among doctors.

His power of concentration was a never-failing source of wonder to those who knew him. One day he was paying his hotel bill in a southern city and when he handed the bills to the clerk he named the amount of each. Some bystanders were greatly astonished to see a blind man handling bills and to hear him naming the amount of each one. He was able to do this because he always kept the different denominations of bills together, but even that required a very retentive memory.

He was never tired of telling others that with the loss of one sense, such as eyesight, other senses became greatly improved. For instance, he pointed out that when he was passing along the street he could generally tell various kinds of stores as he passed by his highly-developed sense of smell. Most people could detect a baker's or delicatessen shop even if their eyes were closed but Doctor Babcock's sense of smell was so keen that he could detect the odors peculiar to furniture, hardware, clothing and many other kinds of stores.

In his laboratory there was an inner room with a carpet and one day he said to his assistant: "How did those ink-stains get into that carpet?" The assistant was greatly surprised. He had not noticed the stains but after a while he found them in the dimly-lighted room. A few days later he said to Doctor Babcock, "Doctor, I hate anything mysterious; it gives me a creepy feeling. However did you know

that there were ink-stains on that carpet?"
The doctor smiled: "Why, I smelt them," he
replied.

In spite of honors and distinctions which
have been showered upon him, Doctor Babcock has remained a singularly modest man.
When, a few years ago, Mr. John Kidder
Rhodes interviewed him in order to tell his
remarkable life story in the *American Magazine* he had great difficulty in getting Doctor
Babcock to say much. "It is not worth talking
about," he said.

When Doctor Babcock does talk he says
that, soon after he became blind, he realized
that the greatest handicap he would have to
face in life would not be that of blindness but
the danger of losing courage, of becoming
sorry for himself. Over and over again, he
has said that nothing worse can befall anyone
than to give way to the spirit of self-pity.
He has never forgotten that night, many years
ago, when his father and mother said good-bye
to him in the Institute for the Blind at Philadelphia. "It seemed hard at the time," he
says, "but it was a wise thing to do and I am
grateful for it." Many long years have passed
since then and Doctor Babcock's long and useful life, his magnificent service to medicine,
prove that he is right.

CHAPTER IX.

A BLACKSMITH WHO BLAZED A TRAIL FOR WORLD PEACE.

ELIHU BURRITT, was the youngest in a family of ten children. He was born at New Britain, Connecticut, on December 8, 1810. Owing to his father's illness, he soon had to shoulder a man's responsibilities and was apprenticed to a blacksmith in the village. Before this, however, an incident happened at school which shows the kind of boy Elihu was.

Those were days when teachers believed that the only way to secure good results in school was by a frequent use of the birch or some other weapon. In the school at New Britain the teacher used a ferrule for punishing the pupils and he had a very unusual way of managing the school. Whenever a pupil was seen misbehaving, he was compelled to stand and hold the ferrule until another pupil was caught; then he passed it to the new culprit. Whoever was holding the ferrule when four o'clock came and school was over, was punished for all who had misbehaved that day. Neither boys nor girls minded having the ferrule during the morning, or early part of the afternoon, but nobody wanted to be holding the instrument of torture as dismissal time drew near.

One day shortly before four o'clock a little girl was caught talking and was given the ferrule. The sight of the girl standing there, and her pitiful expression, was too much for Elihu Burritt; he leaned over to a boy near and began to talk in a loud voice. He was instantly called up and made to take the girl's place. He was severely punished but he did not mind that for he had seen the look of fear on the girl's face and he chose to take the punishment.

Elihu Burritt enjoyed the work of a blacksmith. He toiled early and late; making the smithy ring as his hammer struck the anvil. But he never ceased to regret that he had been compelled to leave school at an early age, and he resolved to improve his education whenever he had a few minutes to spare. He was extremely fond of mathematics and formed the habit of doing sums in mental arithmetic as he worked away at the anvil. For instance, here is one of hundreds of problems he worked out as he swung his hammer: "How many barley corns—three to an inch— will it take to go around the earth at the equator?" He never allowed himself to write anything down when working at these problems.

He became greatly interested in the study of languages. He soon noticed that the languages of different countries closely resembled each other; indeed he used to say that they were like the members of the same family. When he was twenty-one he moved to New Haven in order to be near Yale University and to make use of the library there. Once for a few months he was able to give himself entirely to study, and this is how he divided his time. He rose at four-thirty A.M. and studied German until seven-thirty when breakfast was served. After breakfast he studied Latin and Greek until noon. After dinner he worked on Italian, then went for a short walk. When he returned he took up the study of French, Hebrew and Syraic.

In 1837 friends induced him to set up a grocery store in his native village. But it was a bad year and he had to abandon his store and seek work elsewhere. He walked the entire distance to Boston and, not finding what he wanted there, he pressed on to Worcester and found work in a blacksmith shop. There was a fine library at Worcester and Burritt made good use of it; studying and working in a well arranged manner. After he had been in Worcester for some months he had a fair knowledge of nearly every well-known European language. One day an important will was sent to Elihu Burritt from the West Indies. It was poorly written in Danish, and was so badly spelled and soiled, with several words missing, that no one could make it out, and so the lawyers in their difficulty decided to appeal to Burritt for assistance. It took him several days to decipher the will and unravel the tangle, but he did so to the satisfaction of all concerned. When asked to name his fee, he charged only at the rate per hour of what he would have earned at the anvil.

The study of languages did something for Elihu Burritt that he had never dreamed of at first. It caused him to respect, and even to love, the people of other nations. More and more he came to see that the human race is one family and no matter the color, or nation, or creed they belong to they are really brothers and sisters. Elihu Burritt solemnly resolved that he would devote his life to helping different peoples understand each other and to abolish war as a means of settling disputes.

While living in Worcester he edited a paper named "The Christian Citizen." It was devoted to the support of every good cause. In its pages he advocated temperance, opposed slavery, and encouraged young men and women who wanted to advance their education. But the chief thing about Burritt's paper was that it was the first publication seriously to advocate world peace. Although at first few agreed with him, Elihu Burritt believed that the disputes between nations could be settled by arbitration without the cruel carnage of bloody wars. He persisted in advocating his ideas until he gained supporters, and the self-taught, hard-working blacksmith became as well-known for what were called "his peculiar ideas about war," as he had been for his knowledge of nearly twenty languages.

He visited England in 1846 in order to attend a peace conference. Here he had much to do with forming a new association called, "The League of Universal Brotherhood." In spite of opposition and ridicule, he managed to organize branches of this society in many parts of England, and later had the satisfaction of seeing the movement spread to nearly every country in Europe. New members had to sign a pledge promising to cultivate the spirit of good will towards the people of other nations, and within a year thousands had taken this solemn vow. At one of these meetings a speaker told of standing in an art gallery and looking at a huge painting of a famous battle in British history. It was a ghastly scene with the dead and dying everywhere. A man and his wife, with their boy, drew near. After a while the boy asked: "Father, what was all the fighting about?" The father shook his head and admitted that he did not know. Then the boy appealed to his mother, with the same result. They decided to ask the sergeant-at-arms who was in charge of the room. At the boy's question he seemed more puzzled than either the man or woman. "I'll be hanged if I know what it was all about," he confessed, "but it was a great battle; just look at all the dead men."

Another peace conference was held in Brussels, Belgium, in 1848 with nearly two hundred delegates—drawn from a score of different countries—in attendance. In 1849 the conference was held in Exeter Hall, London, and before a vast audience Elihu Burritt took his place beside many famous orators among whom was the great British statesman, John Bright. By this time Burritt had become known as the outstanding advocate of world brotherhood and when he rose to speak the great gathering, numbering several thousands, gave him a magnificent ovation. He was a plain, modest man with the strong muscles and hard hands of a blacksmith, but the picture of Elihu Burritt standing before that great audience of cheering people, was a proof that the only true greatness in life is that of noble character.

He went to England in 1846 intending to stay a few weeks but he remained three years. When he returned to America in 1849 the people of his native village—New Britain— gave him a wonderful welcome. A few years before he had been a familiar figure there; toiling at the anvil or walking along the village streets. Now he returned a man known and respected on two continents. The town hall was packed to overflowing and half a score of speeches were made by men eager to show their appreciation. Burritt was deeply touched and when he modestly spoke his thanks there were tears in his voice as well as in his eyes.

For more than twenty years Elihu Burritt worked for the establishment of peace and good will among nations. He visited Europe on several occasions and took an active part in organizing peace conferences in Paris, Frankfurt, Edinburgh and many other centers. In 1863 he walked from London to John

O'Groats in the extreme north of Scotland, trudging along with his knapsack on his back and having hundreds of conversations with the folk of the many villages through which he passed. Later he walked from London to Land's End in Cornwall, and back again. He wrote two charming books describing these journeys and the delightful people he met in these travels.

In 1870 Burritt, now a man of sixty, bade farewell to England and returned to America. He retired to his farm at New Britain and spent the closing years of a busy, useful and unselfish life working among his own people. He had devoted more than forty years of his life to worthy causes, and while he did not live to see his suggestions for arbitration fully realized, he had set in motion movements which must eventually reach the goal he had in view.

Elihu Burritt died peacefully on March 6, 1879, at his home in New Britain. Among the many beautiful tributes to his memory, was one by a famous judge who said: "When I was a boy the only way I could secure an education was by long weary walks over the hills to a small schoolhouse; it was the example of Elihu Burritt which gave me ambition to do this."

No doubt hundreds, if not thousands, all over America and in Europe received inspiration as did that judge from the "learned blacksmith's" life. Elihu Burritt did not believe much in inherited genius but he did believe in hard work and perseverance. Over and over again he insisted that he had no special gifts, but that he had trained himself to use every spare moment to advantage and had thus acquired what seemed to be an extraordinary store of knowledge.

After his death Burritt was held up as an example of industry and energy. That a blacksmith, working daily at the forge and anvil, should learn nearly twenty languages was an astonishing achievement and should not be forgotten, but that for which Elihu Burritt will be remembered longest and loved most is the fact that he strove with all his might and main to help men to understand each other; that he blazed a trail for world peace.

CHAPTER X.

ONE day in 1840 an eight-year-old boy walked in a procession through the Austrian city of Hainburg beating a drum. A respected citizen had died and the occasion was an impressive one but the sight of the eight-year-old drummer nearly caused some people to laugh. He was a small boy, too small to carry the drum which had to rest on the back of another boy who was a hunchback. The little drummer was Franz Joseph Haydn; this was his first appearance in public and, though the spectators might be amused, he took his part seriously and felt very important.

Joseph Haydn was the son of Mathias Haydn a wheelwright, who lived in the Austrian village of Rohran, near Vienna. Mathias Haydn also acted as sexton of the church which stood on a hill outside the village. He was a deeply religious man and much respected by all who knew him. He had a good ear for music and each Sunday evening when the duties of the day were finished would bring out his harp, which he had learned to play by ear, and accompany himself in songs and hymns. His wife and their children joined in the singing and every Sunday evening there was a concert in the Haydn home.

When Joseph was a mere infant he saw the village schoolmaster play upon the violin and he never forgot it. At these family concerts, he would get two sticks, using one for the violin and the other for the bow and then, without once taking his eyes off his father, he would play and sing. Mathias Haydn noticed the rapt expression on the boy's face and was greatly interested; to his wife he said: "Some day Joseph will be a great musician."

When Joseph Haydn was eight years of age a distant relative from Hainburg named Johann Frankh visited the Haydn family one evening when they were in the midst of a family concert. The sight of Joseph with his toy violin attracted his attention and the purity and accuracy of the boy's voice convinced him that the little fellow had in him the makings of a musician. He offered to take Joseph to Hainburg and promised that the boy should receive a musical education. The offer was eagerly accepted and in a short time Joseph and his father were seated in their relative's

waggon and jogging on their way to Hainburg.

Johann Frankh, who was a teacher of music,
taught Joseph the art of singing and also gave
him instruction on several musical instruments
of that time. Frankh was a stern man and did
not hesitate to thrash his young relative and often young Joseph was flogged when he ought
to have been fed. The wife of Johann Frankh
was even sterner than he was and seemed to
be very indifferent to the lonely boy who had
hoped to find in her a second mother with the
result that Joseph was neglected in almost
every way. His clothing became shabbier
every day and rents went unmended until
Joseph began to realize that his ragged clothing was attracting the attention of boys with
whom he associated. He noticed that pitying
glances were often cast at him by those who
saw him in the street or as he sat reading on
the steps of his new home.

The one bright spot in Joseph's life at this
time was that he was receiving a good musical
education; music had become the great mas-
tering passion of his life. When he was not
in school he was generally in church listening
to the organ or the singing. He had been admitted to the choir and the music did much to
help him forget his frequent hunger and

shabby clothes.   Then a great event happened in the life of the peasant boy.

In Vienna there was the great St. Stephen's Cathedral and the Capellmeister (choirmaster) visited the church at Hainburg to see if there were any boys there with voices good enough for the cathedral. After a trial he decided to take Joseph Haydn to Vienna with him and the boy's heart fairly leaped within him when he heard the news. His joy soon gave way to grief, however, when he remembered his ragged clothing and poverty-stricken appearance. The Capellmeister whose name was Reutter did not seem to mind this and soon Joseph was singing in the marvellous cathedral at Vienna with its richly-sculptured walls, its stately naves and lofty vaulted roof. It is no wonder that Joseph Haydn wept for joy when first he took his place among the choristers in that magnificent building.

He was twelve years of age when he went to Vienna and had already begun to compose music.   True, his teachers and friends were merely amused at his efforts but he felt he had something within him which he must express and he was forever scribbling on pieces of paper.   He sang in the choir for five years, then his voice began to break and soon the solo parts which had been his were given to other

choristers. Reutter looked for an excuse to
get rid of him and he soon found one. One
day, when the boys sang at the royal court,
the Empress remarked that Joseph Haydn's
voice sounded like the crowing of a rooster.
Soon after that Joseph was dismissed and the
saddest period of his life began.

The morning that Joseph left the comfort-
able quarters of the cathedral home with his
scanty belongings he was almost penniless.
He had never learned any trade; music had
been the great interest of his life. He was
seventeen years of age and he knew he could
not return home as his parents were very poor
and quite unable to help him. He trudged
the streets of the city hungry and weary. Often he stood in the snow-covered streets singing
for a few coppers and during that winter this
was his only means of earning money. More
than once he was near the verge of starvation;
indeed, had it not been for the kindness of a
singer who was himself quite poor, Haydn
would probably have starved to death. This
man took Haydn to his garret where he remained for most of that winter, earning what
little he could by giving violin lessons at very
low rates.

Often he lay in the garret, shivering and
half famished, beneath the scanty coverlet of

his bed almost in despair as he thought of his sad plight. "I will never give up," he said to himself over and over again and soon the tide of his misfortune began to turn a little. He offered to give lessons on the clavier for a few pence and some pupils were attracted. He also secured a few engagements as a violin-player at entertainments and the little he received gave him encouragement. Then something happened which marked a turning-point in his life.

A kind-hearted tradesman named Buchholz, deeply touched by the sight of Haydn's poverty, occasionally engaged him to play to him after business hours. Then, because he liked the boy and believed that he had musical ability he loaned him seventy-five dollars to be returned without interest whenever it suited Joseph. To the starving musician this sum of money seemed a fortune. He rented a small garret and felt as happy as a king. In the next room lived an Italian poet named Metastasio who introduced Haydn to one of the greatest singing masters and composers of that day named Porpora. Haydn offered to clean this man's boots and look after his clothes in return for lessons in music composition. So, for a considerable time, Joseph acted as a valet and whenever he could snatch a few minutes studied how to compose music.

It was a custom in Vienna at that time for struggling musicians to earn a little money by serenading persons of note in the city. There was a distinguished man named Kurz then living in Vienna and it occurred to Haydn and two companions that it might be a good thing to serenade this man and his wife who was a famous beauty. They did so and after a while the door opened and Kurz himself appeared. "Whose music was that you were playing just now?" he asked. "My own," answered Haydn. "Indeed" said the astonished Kurz, "will you please step inside?" Haydn and his companions did so and Kurz, who was manager of Vienna's most beautiful music hall made an appointment with Haydn for the following day. As a result of this man's interest and friendship Haydn was introduced to many musical people who recognized his great ability as a composer and director of music.

About this time a countess who was a patron of music sent for Haydn in order to express her appreciation of some of his work she had heard. Haydn was still quite poor and shabby and when he entered the room of the countess she could scarcely believe that he was so gifted a composer and yet so poor. He told her the story of his bitter struggles and as she listened her eyes filled with tears as she was both kind and generous. In 1759 he was appointed leader of the orchestra of a rich nobleman and with a steady income assured he was able to turn his attention to music composition with a mind freed from worry.

Haydn composed a great deal of church music for he was a deeply religious man. Some complained that his religious music was too cheerful and lacked the solemnity which marked other sacred music. "I cannot help it," said Haydn, "God has given me a cheerful heart and he will surely pardon me if I worship him cheerfully." So this man, whose life had been filled with so much struggle and sorrow refused to be crushed and saddened. Before beginning any composition he earnestly knelt in prayer and asked God to help him in the task.

The fame of Joseph Haydn spread to other lands and later, when he became chief musician to the Prince Nicholas he was often taken, with his entire orchestra, to visit European cities where his ability and charming modest manners, made him a great favorite. In 1791 Haydn decided to accept a pressing invitation to visit England. His close friend, Mozart, tried to dissuade him. "You don't know one word of the language," urged Mozart. To this Haydn replied: "I speak the language of music which is understood all over the world."

England gave Haydn a great reception; everyone seemed anxious to honor one whose music was so greatly loved. Oxford University conferred upon him the degree of Doctor of Music. In London the greatest musicians in the land rendered his music with exquisite skill; more than once he was invited to Buckingham Palace to play for the King and Queen, who expressed the deepest appreciation of his works. Throughout it all he remained simple and unspoiled and it is significant that all great musicians loved him. When the great Beethoven was shown a picture of the cottage where Haydn was born he exclaimed: "To think that so great a man should have been born in a peasant's cottage."

The greatest of all Haydn's compositions is "The Creation" which is now known the world over. It was first given publicly in Vienna on March 19, 1799 and from the first performance it created a profound impression. Few compositions were ever received with such enthusiasm. Some years later, on March 8, 1808, the aged musician expressed a desire to be present at a rendering of "The Creation" which was to be given at Vienna University. He had to be carried into the hall in a chair. The emotions of the vast audience were deeply stirred and when they rose in wild enthusiasm, Haydn simply pointed upwards and devoutly exclaimed: "The music came from above—from God." Haydn died on May 31, 1809, surrounded by those he loved and leaving behind him sweet and noble melodies which have made his name immortal.

CHAPTER XI.

ONE bitterly cold winter's day, a scantily clad negro boy, about seven years old, was walking along the streets of Nashville, Tennessee, when he met an old negro leading a horse. The old man was looking for a mill situated on the edge of the town. The negro boy, whose name was William Deberry, tried to direct the stranger, but at last he gave up in despair. "I will go with you," he said, "if you will let me ride the horse." The old man agreed and in a minute the boy was sitting astride the horse while his playmates looked on with envy and amazement.

William Deberry had forgotten two things: it was bitterly cold, and the mill was about three miles away. The high wind cut like ice, and the little fellow nearly perished. His hands were so cold he could scarcely hold the reins, and he nearly cried with the pain; his toes were absolutely numb. But he had said he would ride to the mill, and though he felt like a frozen lump and his teeth chattered, he got there and danced around to start blood circulation. He walked home and said to his mother, "I'm certainly glad I didn't promise to ride both ways."

A few years later, when he was ten years of age, new streets were being made in his home town of Nashville, and boys were given a chance to break stone for the roadways after school hours. The boy who could break enough to make a pile a foot high and five and a half feet each way, was given fifty cents. William worked every day when school was over for a week, then he was given an order on the paving company for fifty cents. He had to walk nearly three miles to North Nashville to get it cashed, but when he held that half-dollar in his hand there was no happier or prouder boy in all the world. He hurried home as fast as his legs could carry him. "Mother," he shouted breathlessly, "I earned it all myself and it is for you to buy a dress with."

William's mother needed new clothes, and taking the fifty cents she walked to town and bought enough calico with which to make a dress. In after years William remembered that dress well; it seemed to him that his mother had never had such a nice dress and, when she wore it, and he walked beside her, he felt every inch a man.

William went to work when he was fourteen. He "hired out" to a farmer and looked after the horse, did the chores around the farm, helped in the garden, and made himself generally useful. His wages were small but when he received a month's pay he felt that he would never be poor again. He wanted to work in one of the city hotels as a waiter, and probably would have done so had he not met an ambitious young negro who was entering Fisk College. His friendship with this young man made William Deberry realize how little education he had, and he resolved to go back to school and, if at all possible, enter Fisk College. His mother encouraged him, although his father was opposed to the idea.

By determination and perseverance William passed the entrance examination for Fisk, and was admitted as a student. His parents were not in a position to help him very much, so he lost no opportunity of earning a dollar after study hours. For two summers he worked in a sawmill; then he decided that he would take a year off if he could secure a position as a pullman porter and thus save money that he needed badly.

He went to Cincinnati to apply for the position. The president of Fisk College and several other friends had given him letters of introduction, and he felt his chances of getting a position were fairly good. When he got to Cincinnati, however, all the young negroes he met told him it was useless to apply for a porter's place; they had all been turned down.

He presented himself at the office of the Pullman Company. "There's the boss," said the office boy, "he won't give you a job, but there he is." The "boss" was talking with friends at the time and young Deberry knew it would be a mistake to interrupt him and ask for a job, so he walked up to the man's desk, laid his recommendations upon it and quietly stepped back and waited.

After a while the "boss" picked up the papers, read them, then turned to the young negro. "Are you William Deberry?" "Yes, sir." "What do you want?" "A porter's job on a pullman." "Can you fill out an application blank?" "Yes, sir." "Then fill out this one and bring it to me." William did as the man told him and when the "boss" saw how neatly it was done, he said, "I'll take you if you can buy yourself a uniform. It will cost you twenty-five dollars. Can you get it?" "Yes, sir," said William. He only had ten dollars in the world, but he felt sure he could raise the other fifteen. He was given the address of the tailor and he set off at once to find him.

The old tailor was a Jew. William told him his story and showed him his recommendations. "Here are the ten dollars," said the lad, "and I will give you the other fifteen out of my first month's wages."

At first the tailor shook his head. "I never give credit," he said, and William's heart sank. Then the old man read again the letters of reference. He looked at Deberry with penetrating eyes. "I really believe you are an honest boy," he said, "and I am going to take a chance on you since you want an education. Here is the suit."

After a year on the Pullman, William returned to Fisk College and completed his studies. After leaving Fisk he entered Melarsey Medical College in order to study medicine. But he was not very happy for he felt he ought to enter the ministry of the church and help his people. While at Fisk he had listened to an address by an agent of the American Missionary Society. This man pleaded for educated young negroes to enter the ministry. "Many of you find fault with the church and criticize it and the ministers," he said. "Won't you help to make it better?

Will you not give your lives to make it better?"

There and then Deberry decided to become a minister. He left the medical college and entered Oberlin Theological School. He preached at a little church on Sundays and so worked his way through to graduation.

After graduation he was asked to take charge of a small congregation in Springfield, Massachusetts, where the pastor had just died. The church had less than one hundred members, and it was not intended to have Deberry remain for more than a few weeks. But St. John's Church grew and the congregation asked the young man to remain as their pastor. They wanted a married minister, although they had no parsonage. William Deberry went back to Tennessee and married the girl who was waiting for him. She also was a graduate of Fisk College, and the two returned to Springfield where the delighted people built a parsonage for them.

William Deberry went to the little church in Springfield intending to remain a few weeks. He has been there *thirty years* and to write an account of what this splendid negro minister has done for his people would require a book in itself. Church and Sunday School attendance grew so that in a short time St.

John's was one of the largest congregations in Springfield.

Invitations to become their pastor came from larger congregations to Doctor Deberry, so he told his people at Springfield that he would remain as their pastor only on one condition: they must undertake a greater service to the colored community at Springfield. He wanted a church that would be open seven days a week; a church that would be a great center for the life of the people.

The St. John's congregation agreed to Doctor Deberry's proposals and they have worked with him hand in hand, carrying out his great plans with the best of good will. There is now a splendid modern church with a beautiful organ. Doctor Deberry must be a happy man for his church has all the equipment that he desires. There are large comfortably furnished parlors and rest rooms for his people. There are spacious reading rooms and the building is a sub-station of the public library. Hundreds of people, both young and old, are enrolled in various clubs under expert leadership. Clubs for boys and young men have flourished from the beginning, and scores of young negroes in Springfield and the surrounding country have looked to Doctor Deberry for help and advice, and the big-hearted minister has never for one moment forgotten the time when he was sorely in need of help himself.

A farm of fifty-four acres was left to the church some years ago. An agricultural expert was put in charge and groups of men and boys have been enabled to spend delightful vacations there each year. The guests work on the farm in the mornings, and have the remainder of the day for amusement and recreation.

With all this going on Doctor Deberry has never lost sight of the fact that the main purpose of the church is to build character. A census showed recently that there are more young men and women, more boys and girls in St. John's than in any other church in Springfield. When a survey of church work was made by the Inter-Church World Movement, this is the report given of St. John's Church: "This church has the most efficient organization of any church in the group surveyed—regardless of race or denomination."

Such a great work has not been carried on without a tremendous amount of hard work on the part of the energetic and unselfish minister. Doctor Deberry has enjoyed the confidence and respect of the people, both white and colored. On one occasion he approached a prominent white man, Mr. Beebe, and asked him for a two hundred dollar subscription for a particular need. Mr. Beebe gave the minister a thousand dollars saying: "Doctor Deberry, I am interested in your work, but I am more interested in you."

When one great man was asked the secret of his success, he said: "God has always had all there was of me." That is true of William Deberry. He has done a score of things, and done them well. He has broken stones; worked on a farm and in a sawmill. He has been a waiter in hotels and a porter on the railway. To-day he is a Trustee of Fisk University, and one of the most distinguished leaders of his people on the North American Continent.

CHAPTER XII.

HE VALUED HIS SPARE MOMENTS.

ONE afternoon in 1877 a young man, who was a traveller in the grocery business with headquarters at Bolton, England, had finished his usual calls for that day. He looked at his watch; it was just half-past three. He was entitled to spend the next hour and a half as he chose; nearby there were billiard rooms and several other places of amusement. This young man, whose name was William Hesketh Lever, decided to push on to a town named Ince which he had never visited before and where his firm had never done any business.

The first call he made was fruitless. He promptly entered another grocery store and there he obtained an order for three-quarters of a hundredweight of sugar, not a large order, but a beginning. He then called at two more stores and booked an order in each. A fifth grocer did not wish anything but as it was now five o'clock young Lever turned homewards well satisfied with the orders he had received and this town was placed upon his list of regular calls.

When he called at Ince two weeks later he secured new customers; indeed his business connection there grew so that a whole day had to be devoted to that town every two weeks. From Ince the business spread to the nearby town of Wigar with which Lever was destined to have much to do in years to come.

William Hesketh Lever was born at Bolton in Lancashire on September 13, 1851.   His father was a grocer, and as six sisters had been born into the family before him, the new baby boy was given a warm welcome.   As soon as he was old enough, William began to work for his father and as the store was small and little help could be engaged, the boy had to make himself generally useful.   He took down the shutters each morning, swept the floors, cleaned the windows, kept the shelves tidy and delivered parcels to customers.

It may seem a strange choice but the work which William Lever enjoyed more than anything else was that of cutting up and wrapping soap.   Later on he used to say: "I don't know if there was soap in my blood but I loved to handle it and that has remained my favorite occupation."

When William Lever became engaged to be married his salary was five dollars a week. He had, however, great ambition and he knew how to value every spare moment. He made himself so useful that in 1872 his father took him into his business which became known as Lever and Company. Among other commodities sold by the firm was a special brand of soap which was named: "Lever's Pure Honey Soap." William Lever decided to give special attention to making and selling this soap but he did not care for the name. He spoke to a friend about it and this man scribbled several suggestions on a slip of paper. One of these was the name "Sunlight Soap." It flashed across young Lever's mind that this was the very word he wanted and from that day his soap became known as "Sunlight Soap."

His father did not at first encourage William, in fact he opposed the idea. "A cobbler should stick to his last," he said, "be content to work at the grocery business and don't give so much attention to soap." However when William Lever decided to buy a small soap factory at Warrington his father loaned him some money. He began the business in fear and trembling. The people from whom he bought the factory had lost money and his friends prophesied that he would soon be ruined.

Lever had to work very hard himself. He

used to say that he was advertising manager, cashier and sales manager all rolled into one. He was never ashamed to do the hardest or the dirtiest work, with the result that visitors to the factory seldom recognized him. On one occasion a Government inspector walked in and asked to be shown over the premises. Lever told him that if he would wait a moment he would take him around. "That won't do," said the man officiously, "I must have someone different from you to show me around." If there was one thing more than another that Lever detested it was snobbishness and this remark annoyed him. Turning to the Government official, he said: "If you don't go round with me, you will not go at all." The inspector became angered and was soon shown to the door. "He did not know who I was," said Lever, "but that does not excuse him for being insolent."

From boyhood days William Lever had been a very early riser and this habit he retained as long as he lived. He would get up promptly at half-past four in the morning, take a cold plunge in the bath and by five o'clock he was ready to begin the day's work. As he became older it became his custom to sleep for fifteen or twenty minutes after lunch, but he never altered his habit of rising at four-thirty in the morning.

It was in 1885—when he was just thirty-four—that Lever bought the little soap factory and for a while he was not sure whether or not it would succeed. He had put all his own money into the business, beside that which his father had loaned him. He spent two hundred and fifty dollars in advertising and waited for results. Several customers sent the soap back, they didn't like it, and his heart sank. But one day a woman walked into the warehouse and said: "I want some more of that stinking soap; it is good." The woman's remark convinced Lever that the soap must be good and he took new courage.

The business began to grow rapidly. At first the amount of soap manufactured was twenty tons a week; at the end of the first year the output had risen to one hundred and fifty tons weekly and the factory was three months behind with orders. The following year an output of two hundred and fifty tons was reached and within another twelve months this had risen to four hundred and fifty tons.

Lever soon saw that he must have a new and a much larger site. After a careful survey he selected fifty-two acres on the banks of the river Mersey and here he began to build

an immense factory and a village which is
known the world over as "Port Sunlight." He
had made sure that the water supply and railway facilities were ideal with the result that
Port Sunlight is a model village in every respect. Of the fifty-two acres, less than half is
taken up by the factories and offices, the remainder being used for the charming cottages
where the workers live.

Lever had often been saddened as he looked
at the miserable, squalid homes, where most
working people had to live; he determined to
plan and build a village for his employees
where there would be no slums, where every
cottage had its own garden, and every possible
comfort which might be reasonably desired.
The first sod was turned in 1888 and since its
completion in 1890 thousands of social workers and reformers drawn from nearly every
country on earth, have visited Port Sunlight
and Lever's enterprise has received world-
wide praise.

The soap manufactured at Port Sunlight
became known the world over and the Lever
business grew by leaps and bounds.   Lever
visited Canada, the United States, South
Africa and Australia; in each country, factories were opened. When he met the Mayor
and Alderman of Toronto to discuss the pos-

sible purchase of a site they offered him exemption from taxation. There was another soap manufacturer in Toronto, named John Taylor. "Will you give the same exemption to John Taylor?" asked Lever. The city officials said that it was unnecessary as Taylor was well-established. "I am sorry," said Lever, "but I cannot accept tax-exemption which is not equally granted to other soap-manufacturers." The officials appreciated his frank speaking and eventually a settlement was reached which was satisfactory to all.

Lever's business spread to most of the European countries. Soon there were large and flourishing concerns in France, Germany, Switzerland, Holland, and Belgium. In Switzerland Lever announced a great washing competition to take place in Lake Geneva. Hundreds of washerwomen from the different towns along the lake were invited and two of the largest steamers had to be chartered to carry all the competitors. After the contest a great banquet was served at which all the washerwomen were Lever's guests.

It was an advantage to William Lever that he began life on the lowest rung of the ladder. Even when he became one of the best known and most successful business men in the world he never forgot the time when he swept floors, cleaned windows, delivered parcels and wrapped up soap. He was always fair and square and kindly in all his dealings with his employees. The chief ambition of every man who worked for him was to please him and make good in his estimation. When he did rebuke men, it was always done in a tone of disappointment rather than anger. He simply made the guilty ones feel that they had let him down.

His whole business was carried on in a new spirit. He invited all who worked for him to become his partners. He instituted a plan of profit sharing by which all employees could invest their savings with the firm and share in its success. This plan has so encouraged thrift that to-day there are over 18,000 employees who are co-partners, holding stock in the company to the value of nearly fifteen million dollars. In addition to this, employees have been given free insurance policies to the value of over five million dollars.

It would require a book in itself to tell about Port Sunlight which has become known as "The Garden City." With its clean well-kept gardens and lawns it is one of the most picturesque villages in the world, although it is built at the very doors of huge factories. There are magnificently equipped schools,

community halls, social clubs, libraries and
art galleries for the use of the workers. There
is a fine gymnasium and a large open-air
swimming bath. The village has its own
orchestra and choral society, organizations so
good that they have given concerts not only
in many parts of England but in other European countries.

Many great honors came to William Lever.
He was made a baronet in 1911 and became
Sir William Lever; in 1917 he was created
Lord Leverhulme and in 1921, Viscount
Leverhulme. In March, 1914, King George
and Queen Mary visited Port Sunlight. They
entered several of the cottages and expressed
their astonishment and delight at the very way
in which the great manufacturer had fulfilled
his ideals for working people.

William Lever—or Viscount Leverhulme
as he was then—died at London on May 7,
1925, at the ripe age of eighty-four. His body
was taken to Port Sunlight where thousands
of people paid their tributes of affection and
respect. His life was a remarkable example
of how a great business man may carry into all
he does, a spirit of gentleness, kindness, and
consideration for others, and of how much
genuine happiness it is possible for a good man
to bring into the lives of other people.

CHAPTER XIII.

IN 1811 a boy just over fifteen years of age entered Harvard University. This boy, whose name was William Hickling Prescott was born at Salem, New England, on May 4, 1796, and his fine record at school had caused his parents to expect great things from him. He had only been a few weeks at Harvard when an accident happened which changed his whole life. One day after dinner several students were having a frolic and one of them threw a hard crust of bread across the room which struck William Prescott full in the eye. He was not taking part in the fun but happened to be passing just at the moment when the missile was thrown.

The blow had an unusual effect. His strength completely left him and he fell to the ground in great pain. His pulse became so feeble that although is mind was clear he was unable even to sit up and his parents became alarmed. He was taken home and the family physician, Dr. James Jackson, was called. He pronounced the affliction, "deep paralysis of the retina" and in spite of all that was done the sight of the eye was completely lost. He was compelled to spend many weary months in a darkened room, for even a softened light caused him intense pain, but he never once gave up hope of returning to college and eventually his wish was gratified and he took his place among the students again.

One effect of the accident was to make him a better student than ever. During the long months of confinement in his room he had been compelled to think a great deal. His mother and others read to him and he remembered every word, indeed he developed an extraordinary memory. Later his memory became so retentive that after listening to someone reading sixty pages of a book he could give a synopsis of the reading, often quoting entire passages without making a single mistake.

When he returned to college his memory was so good that when studying mathematics —a subject he disliked and never mastered— he could commit a whole problem to memory, answer included, without really understanding it. As a result he secured good marks in examinations although he said he was a dunce in the subject. He explained his position to the teacher of mathematics who was amazed at Prescott's marvellously retentive memory.

His unfortunate accident had not dampened his cheerful disposition. Of all the merry-hearted students in Harvard, William Prescott was the leader and more than once his love of fun nearly got him into trouble. Sometimes he was seized with uncontrollable laughter and these fits often came over him when he wanted to be most serious. On one occasion he was given a part to play in Shakespear's drama, "Julius Cœsar" but at the rehearsals he burst out laughing at the most serious moments and, do what he could, he was unable to restrain his merriment and another had to take his place.

Elocution was one of his subjects at college and here his sense of humor often overcame him. Once when alone with the teacher of elocution the funny side of the situation so struck him that he laughed in spite of the fact that the teacher was plainly annoyed. At first the teacher felt that Prescott's behavior was an insult; however, after a while he began to laugh himself and soon he was as helpless as his pupil. For a while neither could speak but at last the teacher managed to say: "Prescott, the lesson is over."

William Prescott graduated from Harvard

with honors in 1814 and began to work in his father's law office. Before long his good eye became inflamed and he consulted Dr. Jackson who ordered leaches to be placed on his temple in order to subdue the inflammation. For a while the pain raged furiously and it seemed certain that Prescott would never see again. For sixteen weeks he remained in a darkened room, unable to walk a step and every day suffering intense pain. During these days his patience and good nature were remarkable; if he ever felt discouraged he managed to conceal it.

One result of this sickness was to impair, not only the sight of his remaining eye, but also his general health, so when he recovered he went to visit some relatives at St. Michael's in the Azores. Here again he was attacked by inflammation in his eye and lived for six weeks in a room so dark that he could not even see the furniture. He managed to get necessary exercise by walking with his arms extended so that he would not bump into things. He said that during this confinement he must have walked hundreds of miles with his arms outstretched.

In April, 1816, he sailed for England where he arrived after a trying voyage of twenty-four days. He hastened to consult Sir William

Adams, one of the most famous oculists in the world, but Sir William could do little for him except advise him to have others read to him instead of trying to read himself. From England he went to Italy, and then to Germany, returning to the United States in 1817. About this time he wrote an article and sent it with high hopes to the *North American Review* magazine but it was rejected.

In May 1820 Prescott was married and in the same year he decided upon literature as a profession. Although he had only partial sight in one eye, and was totally blind in the other, his remarkable memory enabled him to retain what he did read and to remember what others read to him. He engaged readers and constructed a device which enabled him to make notes as the reading proceeded. These notes were read to him later and in that way he began to write his remarkable histories. He was fortunate in finding a well educated young man, Mr. James English, who read to him for six hours every day during four years; indeed from that time, until the close of his life some thirty years later, he was never without the services of a reader. His secretary, Mr. English, has left an unforgettable picture of Prescott at work. For hours he would remain in his room, surrounded by green screens; the windows covered by dark blue curtains. Often he was in great pain but there was no trace of it in his face, nor in his voice. For several years he studied Spanish history and his first great work was: "The History of the Reign of Ferdinand and Isabella." The book was well received; its accuracy and interesting style commended it to students. In December 1843, Prescott completed his "History of The Conquest of Mexico," and three years later followed this with a "History of Peru." All his books bore the stamp of most careful preparation and Prescott's ranks among the greatest historians of the world. When he died he had commenced the third volume of a great work; "The History of Philip II." It is sufficient to say, of all Prescott's books, that upon whatever historical subject he wrote, his books are most accurate.

During the last ten or even fifteen years of his life Prescott was practically blind although he would not admit it. Naturally cheerful he did not want to be pitied. He once said: "Do not think that I feel any despondency. My spirits are as high as my pulse—that is fifteen degrees above normal." When one remembers the intense pain to which he was so frequently subject, together with his almost total blindness, the two amazing things about him were his amazing cheerfulness and his great capacity for hard work.

He was one of the kindest men who ever lived and quite free from any kind of petty spite. He never attached the slightest blame upon the person who had been the means of his becoming blind, in fact, he went out of his way to show the man a kindness and made it clear that in his heart he had not the slightest hard feeling. He was never known to say a harsh or unkind thing about anyone, and the many secretaries, who read to him loved him. Perhaps his own troubles had made him sympathetic; whatever the reason was he was extremely generous to all who needed assistance and as the enormous sale of his books made him fairly wealthy, he was able to assist many who sought his aid.

His love of fun was irrepressible and other members of the family caught his happy spirit. One day an uncle of his who believed that he was becoming deaf called upon Prescott. The historian insisted that his uncle's deafness was all imaginary and in order to prove it suggested that a watch be placed at one end of a room and that both should approach it slowly and should stop as soon as either heard the watch ticking. "You will hear that ticking as soon as I do," said Prescott, "then you will realize that your hearing is all right for I know mine is good."

Very slowly the two men approaching the watch, advancing only a few inches at a time. "Do you hear it?" asked Prescott. "Not yet," said his uncle. Steadily the couple advanced until they were only a short distance off. "I knew I was deaf," said the uncle, "I cannot hear a thing." "Don't worry," replied Prescott, "I hear nothing myself." When they had their faces less than ten inches away, Prescott's face had a bewildered expression. "I must be getting deaf myself," he groaned. "I cannot hear any ticking; surely I am not going to be both blind and deaf." Finally he got so close that his ear touched the watch—still no sound. Then he fairly yelled, "Why the old watch isn't going!" His wife confessed that she had stopped the watch and that she was nearly convulsed with laughter as the two men strained to hear the ticking of a watch that wasn't going. Then William Prescott had one of his fits of uncontrollable laughing for, while he enjoyed all kinds of fun, he seemed to relish it all the more when the joke was on himself.

So this man of marvellous courage carried on, doing as much work as two or three ordinary men, and ever having a song of gladness in his heart. He once drew up the following set of "Rules for Happiness": Good nature; manliness; independence; industry; honesty; cheerfulness and religious confidence.

William Hickling Prescott passed away quietly in his study on January 28, 1859, surrounded by the books he loved so well. After his death a complete list of his historical works was published in sixteen volumes. When the severe handicaps he had to face are taken into consideration and the very high standard of his books is remembered, the story of Prescott's achievement is one of the most inspiring of the Nineteenth Century.

CHAPTER XIV.

A Mill-Boy Who Became a Cabinet Minister.

ONE summer morning in 1879 a ten-year-old boy set out from his home to begin work in a mill at Oldham in Lancashire, England. There were tears in his mother's eyes as she kissed him good-bye as she understood better than he did what life in the mill would mean but the little fellow, whose name was John Robert Clynes, was thrilled with the thought of being a wage-earner. True the wage was small—less than seventy-five cents a week—but he knew even that much would be a help where there was a large family and little money to provide for them.

The Clynes home was in the poor district of Oldham and his parents though respectable, were quite poor. The boy's father, Patrick Clynes, was a hard-working laborer who had left Ireland hoping to make better wages in the Lancashire cotton mills. A period of depression had resulted in his being thrown out of work and, try as he would he never succeeded in earning more than six dollars a

week and a good part of the time he did not
earn even that much. When John Robert
Clynes—or Jack as he was called by his
chums, began to work there were seven small
children in the home and the total income was
scarcely sufficient to provide food and clothing. Food that was cheap but nourishing was
the best that the children could hope for and
bread and butter became the principal diet.

Jack Clynes saw little of the inside of a
school and what time he did spend there was
never a happy memory. In those days many
schoolmasters thought that every boy ought to
be severely thrashed from time to time and
Jack, who had always been frail and delicate,
soon regarded the school with horror. After
he began to work in the mill Jack Clynes attended school each afternoon until his twelfth
birthday was reached. Perhaps the schoolmaster who, like Jack's father, was an Irishman, had taken a dislike to Jack Clynes but
whatever was the reason scarcely a day passed
without Jack being soundly flogged. For two
years the lad set off early in the morning for
the mill where he worked hard until noon,
then after eating one or two slices of bread
and butter, he went to school.

One afternoon the schoolmaster was even
more irritable than usual and the thing which

roused his anger that day was that, for some reason unknown to him, Jack Clynes seemed to be very happy. He thrashed him with the cane but while Jack's lips twitched, his eyes danced with glee. The day was hot, the schoolmaster was a stout man and he laid on the cane until he was exhausted.

Puffing and perspiring at last he laid it down and with a puzzled expression said to Jack: "John Robert Clynes, what imp of Satan possesses ye?" "No imp at all," said Jack, "but it's me that possesses a birthday and—*it's my twelfth.*" Instantly the schoolmaster caught the point. This was to be Jack Clynes' last day in school. So that was why the young rascal was so happy! He reached for the cane,—at least there was time to give Jack one more sound flogging. "John Robert Clynes," he said, "I have utterly failed to make a scholar of ye, but it's my solemn duty to make a man of ye." Instantly there was a clatter of clogs across the floor; Jack escaped and banged the door behind him. A moment later his laughing face appeared at the open window: "It will have to be at the mill that ye'll do the making of me" he fairly yelled. He ran off leaving the schoolmaster furious and his chums greatly amused at the fun although they were afraid to show it. Thus Jack Clynes' schooldays came to an end.

After several years of very hard work in the mills Jack's salary rose to four dollars a week. It was sorely needed at home where there were nine mouths to feed and he gladly gave it to his parents, who allowed him sixteen cents a week for pocket money. By this time Jack realized that it was a terrible handicap to face the world without an education and, though he had no desire to be back with the brutal schoolmaster, he often wished that he had a better education.

One evening, as he was returning from work, his eye rested on a second-hand dictionary. The cost was thirty-five cents and while that meant more than two weeks pocket money he purchased it and carried it home in triumph. There, in his tiny room, by the light of a candle, Jack Clynes began to pour over the pages of his dictionary. Later he bought a grammar for eighteen cents and each evening when his day's work was done he thumbed these two books until overcome by weariness he fell asleep.

Most people find the dictionary uninteresting and seldom use it except when they want to find out the meaning of some word or how to spell one; not so Jack Clynes. He loved the sound of words—especially long ones. When he heard eloquent men speak using words in their proper place it sounded to him like music and although he was never given to "show-off," when anyone asked him the meaning of a word or how to spell it, he was happy if he could help them. Although he had attended school so little he soon taught himself to read clearly and distinctly and he was often asked to read aloud both in his own family and in neighbor's homes.

Not far away from Jack Clynes' home three old blind men lived together. Jack's reputation for reading reached them and they offered him a few coppers a week if he would read the newspapers aloud for them. The generous lad agreed, not so much for the few coppers, but because of the happiness he knew it would bring into the lives of these unfortunate men. Many an hour Jack spent reading to them and although he did not always understand the meaning of it all he could see that the blind men greatly enjoyed it.

Perhaps it was because of their blindness, but these three old men were all thoughtful and it was the political news of the day that they enjoyed most of all. Sometimes they asked Jack to read certain passages two and three times, then they would try to repeat what he had read and more than once Jack was astonished to find that they could repeat it, word for word. This reading had a wonderful effect upon Jack Clynes. It filled his mind with noble thoughts and gave him great interest in the better things of life. At the time he simply thought he was giving pleasure to three unfortunate men; little did he realize that he was laying up treasure for years to come.

By this time Jack Clynes was hungry for knowledge and he was often saddened by the fear that it might be too late. Often he stood for hours outside a bookstall looking in at the window, wondering what book he would buy with the little money he had to spend. He told his blind friends about his ambition and one of them eagerly hastened to introduce him to an old man in the neighborhood who had been a schoolmaster. This old man had a few pupils attending his evening classes and who paid him a small fee. Jack Clynes attended these classes two evenings each week and this, together with the reading he did at home and in the public libraries, soon made him a fairly well-educated young man. He joined a debating society and learned to express his thoughts in public. He had formed a friendship with a young man named Byrne and often the two made their way to an old stone quarry where, in addressing imaginary audiences, they gained in fluency and when they attended meetings where they were asked to speak they astonished others with their oratory.

Naturally enough the things in which Jack Clynes was interested were such as had to do with working people. He had known poverty from his childhood and he was anxious to improve the lot of working people, to see them living in better homes, receiving higher wages and having more time for rest and enjoyment. He began to write letters to the newspapers advocating these reforms and, as he was now a piecer in the mill he used the *nom de plume* "piecer" instead of his own name. For some time no one knew who "piecer" was although the articles were so well written and the arguments so clearly stated that people began to wonder who the writer could be.

When the discovery was made at last Jack Clynes became known as "Piecer Clynes" and his services as a speaker were sought after, not only in Oldham, but throughout the outlying districts. He was glad and eager to help workingmen toward better conditions although he did not receive any money for his services and often even had to pay his own travelling expenses out of a very slender purse.

Many an evening he left the mill and, regardless of food, set off in his working clothes to address a meeting which often meant for him a walk of several miles each way.

When he was twenty-two years of age Jack Clynes was asked to accept the position of paid organizer of The Union of Gas and General workers. He accepted the position and for six years served faithfully; then he was elected secretary of the Union for the Lancashire District, a position he still holds. When he was first elected the Union had a membership of two thousand which has risen to sixty thousand. Promotion did not come easily to him, in fact nothing ever came to him for which he did not have to work hard. Three times he was a candidate for municipal honors in Oldham and each time he was defeated, although he came a little nearer to success each time.

Then in 1906 Jack Clynes was asked to become a candidate for the British House of Commons for the constituency of North-West Manchester and, after some hesitation, he accepted the nomination. Clynes was little known in Manchester and at first it seemed a hopeless fight. He had to overcome a lot of prejudice and meet considerable chaffing and ridicule. One man expressed what others were thinking when he indignantly said: "Only *gentlemen* ought to go to Parliament."

On the night of the election, when the votes were being counted, Jack Clynes walked calmly over to the room where the counting was in progress, but was stopped by a burly policeman who evidently did not recognize him. "Well, my little man," he said to Clynes, "what do you want?" "Oh, nothing very much," said Jack, "only I thought I would like to know what my majority is." The constable was aghast. "Certainly, Mr. Clynes," he said meekly, "Come this way, sir, I am proud to have met you."

John Robert Clynes—to give him his proper name—was elected to the British House of Commons by a substantial majority over his opponent and the mill-boy who had often gone to school, and later to his work, hungry and shabbily clothed, took his place among the men who administer the affairs of the British Empire and became a Cabinet Minister.

During the Great War of 1914-1918 the question of the distribution of food became one of the most serious problems that each nation in turn had to face. John Robert Clynes was appointed Parliamentary Secretary to the Minister of Food, a position somewhat similar

to that held at the same time by Mr. Hoover
in the United States. Clynes filled that difficult position with credit to himself and earned
the gratitude of the whole nation. There was
criticism, of course, as there was of food distribution in all the countries engaged in the
War, but everybody agreed that Clynes was
anxious to be fair and just, and especially
anxious that women and children should receive proper nourishment.

John Robert Clynes was appointed a member of the Cabinet of the Labor Government
when it was elected to office in 1928. He is
still in middle life and all who know him
hope that he may live to see many of his
dreams come true. Physically he has never
been strong but he has a clear brain, a tender
heart and a determination to leave the world
better than he found it.

CHAPTER XV.

A DELICATE MAN WHOSE HYMNS WILL NEVER BE FORGOTTEN.

IT seems strange that one of the greatest hymnwriters who ever lived, one whose inspiring hymns are sung by millions every week, was a little man so frail and delicate that his life was often despaired of. His name was Isaac Watts and he was born at Southampton, England, in July, 1674. As a baby he was sick and puny, and throughout life he remained so small in stature that he seemed little more than a dwarf.

He was born at a time when there was a great deal of religious persecution and when he was only a few days old his father was thrown into a dark and unwholesome prison cell because of his religious convictions. When Isaac was a mere baby he was often carried by his mother to a seat near the prison door, and there the unhappy woman remained waiting for a chance to comfort her imprisoned husband. Although Isaac's father was a man of noble character, he was thrown into prison so frequently that the boy's life, as well as that of his mother, was saddened by the hardships of those days.

Even as a boy of ten or eleven, Isaac Watts could write the most astonishing poetry. One morning, while all the members of the houshold were on their knees at morning prayers, young Isaac was heard to titter. As soon as devotions were over, his father sternly demanded to know the reason of the unseemly giggling. Isaac nervously pointed to a bell-rope hung by the fireplace. "I saw a little mouse run up that rope during prayers," he said, "and these lines came into my head:

> *There was a mouse for want of stairs,*
> *Ran up a rope to say his prayers.*

The father, without another word, turned to a shelf and took down a rod, whereupon young Isaac begged, with tears streaming down his eyes:

> *Oh father, father, pity take*
> *And I no more will verses make.*

The boy's father was so impressed with Isaac's poetic gift that he laid down the rod with a puzzled expression on his face. However, neither his father or mother wished to destroy the tiny boy's love for rhyming and often his mother used to offer half-a-cent to any member of the family who could compose the best rhyme and Isaac was always the winner.

In those days it was not easy even for an ambitious boy to secure an education, but Isaac had a hunger for knowledge and applied himself to his studies with amazing perseverance. He formed the habit of studying far into the night and this, together with the fact that he was naturally delicate, brought on more than one breakdown in health. When he was a little over twenty, Isaac obtained a position as tutor in the family of Sir John Hartopp. The work suited him well; he had a natural talent for teaching and he loved the work. During these happy years he found time to write religious poetry, and also to preach occasionally. In 1699, when he was twenty-five, he became assistant to Rev. Dr. Chauncery who was pastor of a large congregation in London.

As a pastor, Isaac Watts was greatly loved by the congregation although his health was such that for days, often for weeks at a time, he was confined to his room. When, because of advancing years, Dr. Chauncery retired, Isaac Watts became minister in his place, and his eagerness to serve the people made such demands upon his strength that from time to time he was completely prostrated. When these ailments came it was his custom to write pastoral letters which were read to the congregation, and the tenderness and courage of the chronic sufferer were a constant source of wonder to the congregation. Even when he was racked with pain, Isaac Watts managed to maintain a peace of mind and calmness which breathes in all his hymns.

Few people who sing the hymns of Isaac Watts will ever know the circumstances under which many of them were written. Here and there, however, the effect of his sickness is seen. In 1706 the condition of his health was such that he went to Southampton for rest and change. One day while there he gazed across the gulf to smiling fields beyond, and one of his most beautiful hymns was composed at that time. The first verse, especially, reveals the longing of this much tried sufferer:

There is a land of pure delight
Where saints immortal reign;
Infinite day excludes the night,
And pleasures banish pain.

In spite of his sickness, no other man did more to make public worship bright and inspiring than Isaac Watts. The church services of his day were often so solemn as to be depressing. The congregation sang psalms only, and the tunes were generally dull and lifeless. One day Isaac was returning from a service with his father when he bitterly complained about the singing. "Why don't you try to compose something better?" said his father. It was this thought which first started him to write hymns for congregational singing, and from that day until his death many years after, he continued to write hymns and to-day a larger number of his hymns are in constant use than of any other hymn-writer.

In 1707 Watts published his "Hymns and Spiritual Songs." Nothing like it had ever appeared before and while many welcomed the hymns, others were bitterly opposed to their use. In the introduction to the volume Watts frankly gave his reasons for writing the hymns and publishing them. He said that as he stood in the pulpit and looked into the faces of the congregation when the psalms were being sung, he could not fail to notice how utterly indifferent and bored most of the congregation were. He was a great lover of boys and girls and he particularly noticed how fidgety and restless they appeared during the singing of psalms set to impossible tunes. These things had convinced him that there was great need of hymns that old and young could sing heartily and thoroughly enjoy.

Some of the best-known hymns written by Isaac Watts are: "Come, let us join our cheerful songs;" "Jesus shall reign where'er the sun;" "O God our help in ages past;" "Before Jehovah's awful throne;" "When I survey the wondrous cross;" "From all that dwell beneath the skies;" "Come, Holy Spirit, heavenly dove;" "Sweet fields beyond the swelling flood," and "Alas and did my Saviour bleed." It is said that at the present time there are no less than seventy hymns composed by Isaac Watts in constant use. During the Great War of 1914-18 there was no more popular hymn with the soldiers than the magnificent one beginning:

> *O God, our help in ages past,*
> *Our hope for years to come;*
> *Our shelter from the stormy blast,*
> *And our eternal home!*

The hymns introduced by Isaac Watts made a great change for the better in church services. From being careless and indifferent, congregations began to take great interest in the singing. The very pews seemed to vibrate with the fervor of the people, and the flickering candles which stood up from the little round holes in the pew tops would start as if with alarm and quite frequently go out.

In 1714 Isaac Watts was again in such poor health that a wealthy gentleman, Sir Thomas Abney, invited him to spend a week with him at his country home in Hertfordshire. Watts went and fell in love with the lovely home and its country surroundings. His blanched cheeks regained their natural color and his thin wasted little body revived; something else happened. The Abney family fell in love with Isaac Watts. His charming personality, his gracious, modest bearing and his patience under great suffering so endeared him to this family that although invited to stay with them for a week, he remained with them during the remainder of his life. And so this charming little man, who went to stay with the Abneys for one week, *remained thirty-four years*. Many great honors came to Isaac Watts. The Universities of Edinburgh and Aberdeen both conferred upon him the degree of Doctor of Divinity, and his fame as a hymn-writer went everywhere.

In appearance Watts was so small as to be almost insignificant. This was a constant grief to him and a subject upon which he was very sensitive. On one occasion he was standing near a coffee-house with some friends when he overheard a gentleman ask the name of "that odd-looking little man." When his question was answered, the gentleman exclaimed in a loud voice: "What, is that the great Dr. Watts?" This was too much for the sensitive hymn-writer. Quoting a passage from one of his own poems entitled, "False Greatness," he said:

Were I so tall to reach the pole,
  Or grasp the ocean with my span,
I must be measured by my soul,
  The mind's the measure of the man.

It was said of Watts, however, that no matter what company he was in, his conversation made others forget all about his personal appearance; he was a giant in mind and soul.

Isaac Watts lived in days when there was a good deal of religious bitterness and persecution, but he remained one of the kindest and gentlest men who ever lived. Nowhere in any of his works, or in any of the anecdotes recorded of him, is there to be found one angry remark about another. Although he never married, he was especially fond of children, and wrote many poems and hymns for their use.

He died on the afternoon of November 25, 1748, and was buried in Bunhill Fields Ceme-

tery, not far from the resting-place of Susha-
nah Wesley, and within a few steps of the
grave of Daniel Defoe, author of *Robinson
Crusoe*. No one would have thought that the
tiny baby, born in 1674, would live to pass his
eighty-fourth birthday, but he did so and millions of people are grateful for his noble life.

Lamplighter Rare Collector's Series

The Basket of Flowers. CHRISTOPH VON SCHMID
First written in the late seventeen hundreds, this book is the first in the **Lamplighter Collector's Series** which gave birth to Lamplighter Publishing. Come to the garden with the godly gardener, James, and his lovely daughter, Mary, and you will see why Elisabeth Elliot and Dr. Tedd Tripp so highly recommend this rare treasure.

Titus: A Comrade Of The Cross. F. M. KINGSLEY
In 1894 the publisher of this book gave a $1,000 reward to any person who could write a manuscript that would set a child's heart on fire for Jesus Christ. In six weeks, the demand was so great for this book that they printed 200,000 additional copies! You and your family will fall in love with the Savior as you read this masterpiece.

A Peep Behind The Scenes. O. F. WALTON
Behind most lives, there are masks that hide our hurts and fears. As you read, or more likely cry, through this delicate work, you will understand why there is so much joy in the presence of angels when one repents. Once you read it, you will know why two-and-a-half-million copies were printed in the 1800s.

Jessica's First Prayer. H. STRETTON
What does a coffee maker have in common with a barefoot little girl? You will want to read this classic over and over again to your children as they gain new insights into compassion and mercy as never before.

Stepping Heavenward. ELIZABETH PRENTISS
Recommended by Elisabeth Elliot, Kay Arthur, and Joni Eareckson Tada, this book is for women who are seeking an intimate walk with Christ. Written in 1850, this book will reach deeply into your heart and soul with fresh spiritual insights and honest answers to questions that most women and even men would love to have settled.

Joel: A Boy of Galilee. ANNIE FELLOWS JOHNSTON
If you read *Titus: A Comrade of the Cross* and loved it, let me introduce you to Joel. This is a story about a handicapped boy who has to make a decision whether to follow the healer of Nazareth or the traditions of the day. This is a treasure you will talk about for years.

Jessica's Mother. H. STRETTON AND M. HAMBY

(sequel to Jessica's First Prayer)

Rewritten by Mark Hamby, this sequel will take you through the emotions of the greatest of all sacrifices. Embittered against God and anyone who bears the name of Christ, Jessica's mother is determined to take her daughter back regardless of the consequences. This is a story of human tragedy and divine love that will inspire families to take a second look at the real meaning of the gospel of Jesus Christ.

Christie's Old Organ. O.F. WALTON

This is a child's story for all ages. Join a little boy named Christie and an old organ grinder as they search for the path that leads to heaven. This is a dramatic story that has already led children to the saving knowledge of Jesus Christ. Be prepared to cry.

The Inheritance. CHRISTOPH VON SCHMID

This is another classic by the author of *The Basket of Flowers*. Seeking first the Kingdom of God and His righteousness will be a theme that parents and children will see through the eyes of a faithful grandson and his blind grandfather.

The Lamplighter. MARIA S. CUMMINS

Written in the 1800's when lamplighters lit the street lights of the village, this story will take you on a spiritual journey depicting godly character that will inspire and attract you to live your Christian life with a higher level of integrity and excellence. Mystery, suspense, and plenty of appealing examples of integrity and honor will grip the heart of anyone who reads this masterpiece.

The Hedge of Thorns. ANONYMOUS

Based on a true story about a little boy who will do almost anything to find out what is on the other side of a hedge of thorns. Enticed and frustrated, a child is about to learn why boundaries are a necessary part of God's plan for his life.

Mary Jones and Her Bible. ANONYMOUS

Another true story of a little girl whose strongest desire in life is to possess her very own Bible. Through hard work, determination, prayer, faith, and even a sixty mile walk, Mary Jones will do whatever it takes to obtain a copy of the Word of God. This true story will not only kindle a fire in children's hearts but give them a role model to follow that exemplifies hard work, faithfulness, and the reward of patient obedience.

The White Dove. CHRISTOPH VON SCHMID

This is another classic by the author of *The Basket of Flowers* that will once again lay a beautiful pattern of godliness for all to follow. Surrounded by knights and nobles, thieves and robbers, this story will take parent and child to the precipice of honor, nobility, sacrifice, and the meaning of true friendship. If you enjoyed *The Basket of Flowers*, you will not want to miss *The White Dove*.

Mothers of Famous Men. ARCHER WALLACE

Take a step back in time and visit with the great mothers of great men. Join Mrs. Washington, Mrs. Wesley, Mrs. Franklin, Mrs. Adams, Mrs. Lincoln, Mrs. Carnegie and many others and see what type of motherhood shaped such unusual greatness. You will enter their homes as well as their hearts, as you learn for the first time, portions of history rarely revealed. This is a book every mom, dad, and young person needs to read.

Clean Your Boots, Sir? ANONYMOUS

Finally, a book for boys that I would say equals *The Basket of Flowers*! In this captivating story you will meet a brave little boy who cares for his ailing father and two baby brothers. As a shoeshine boy, the little savings that he makes each day is just enough to meet their basic needs until a small act of honesty changes his life forever. Join the shoeshine boy as he introduces your children to integrity, honesty, faith, and sacrifice, in a way that they will never forget!

Melody, The Story of A Child. LAURA E. RICHARDS

An inspiring and beautifully written story that invites the reader to see life through the eyes of a most unusual child. Each chapter is filled with charming freshness as a blind child weaves her gift of "seeing" into the hearts of friend and foe alike. Themes: uncompromising love, discernment, childlike honesty, faith and forgiveness.

The Lost Ruby. CHRISTOPH VON SCHMID

Another classic that will teach children the important lesson of honesty regardless of the cost. Also included is one of Von Schmid's finest short stories, **The Lost Child**. This is a story that is filled with mystery and intrigue as the reader learns that God allows hardships for our good.

The Little Lamb. CHRISTOPH VON SCHMID

This story will teach our readers that all things do work together for good to them who love God. Parents and children will be filled with captivating suspense as they taste and see that the Lord is the God of the impossible.

True Stories of Great Americans for Young Americans. ANONYMOUS

Written for young readers, this edition of American history will inspire and reveal the character qualities and difficult circumstances that led these Americans to greatness. The seldom heard stories of George Washington, Robert E. Lee, Patrick Henry and many more will inspire and challenge young readers to value the past and guard the present as they themselves become agents of change for the future.

Boys of Grit Who Became Men of Honor, ARCHER WALLACE

Children and adults will be inspired when they read about boys who overcame great misfortunes, trials, and overwhelming circumstances to become great and godly men. When so many others saw only difficulties, they saw possibilities.

The Three Weavers. ANNIE FELLOWS JOHNSTON

Fathers and daughters will take a journey back to Camelot and learn the unforgettable lessons of virtue and vice.

The Stolen Child. CHRISTOPH VON SCHMID

Another Von Schmid classic that captures the beauty of God's creation as seen through the eyes of a child who lived in darkness most of his childhood. Lessons of responsibility and forgiveness are among the many virtues taught in this classic.

Always in His Keeping. ANONYMOUS

Based on a true story during the time of John Wesley, a brother and sister who are stolen as infants struggle to find their true identity and the faith to rest in a God who sometimes allows the righteous to suffer.

The Pillar of Fire. J.H. Ingraham

This is the most eloquently written, filled with the most illustrative accounts of the Prince of Tyre during his visit to Egypt over 3500 years ago. The author brings full color and inspiration to every page, while weaving his most suspenseful dramas in connection with the Scriptures. Truly, a fresh breath of literary air.

Rosa of Linden Castle. CHRISTOPH VON SCHMID

In this unique Von Schmid classic, a daughter's love for her condemned father will inspire children of all ages to see that though it was meant for evil, God always intends it for good.

Stick to the Raft. MRS. GEORGE GLADSTONE

I am excited to present Stick to the Raft because the wonderful lessons of honesty, mercy, perseverance, and integrity are skillfully woven by a master story teller. This is a story that children will never forget. Young and old alike will enjoy taking a journey with a poor boy who is honored for his hard work and honesty. However, just when things were going so well, misfortune, which was really disguised as the providence of God, entered his life as he became the target for mischief among jealous peers. Children and young adults will learn the important lessons that there is no fear in love, and that forgiveness and truth are the greatest healers of all.

Christie: the King's Servant . O.F. WALTON

In the sequel to Christie's Old Organ, we find Christie pastoring a small parish in New England, where a forgotten acquaintance steps back into his life. Here in this quaint village where fisherman take to their boats for a living, there is intense drama each time the clouds and winds begin to blow. Filled with delicate love and unusual hospitality, each reader will be moved with compassion when Duncan's boat is found battered and empty days after the search has ended. Loss is never easy but this is one loss our readers will never forget!

The Golden Thread. N. MACLEOD; rewritten by M Hamby

There was once a kingdom that existed near the treacherous Hemlock forest where an evil king and his followers dwelt. Citizens knew that only those who held the Golden Thread could wander past the boundaries of the kingdom and return safely. It is a fearful thing to lose one's way, especially in the dark forest. And no one knows this better than Prince Phillip, who must learn the lessons of the golden thread if he is ever to return.

Stephen: A Soldier of the Cross. FLORENCE KINGSLEY

The long awaited sequel to Titus is finally here! When I first began reading Stephen I was expecting a similar story, but to my surprise the author eloquently and skillfully created another masterpiece. Starting in the deserts of Egypt, a blind sister and her powerful brother, find themselves the target of slave traders. After hearing the reports of miracles in Jerusalem, they flee for their lives and find themselves in the midst of the greatest, most life-changing event in history. But will it be too late for the blind girl? Readers will find themselves engulfed in this intense drama that unfolds at the foot of the cross.

Teddy's Button. AMY LEFEUVRE

Here's a story that will warm your heart, make you laugh, and above all, will help children to understand the spiritual battle that rages in their souls. Join Teddy as he demonstrates that even a child can enlist in God's army and carry the banner of love and victory high.

The Beggar's Blessing. MARK HAMBY

A true story from the 1800s about a little girl who sacrificed her savings for a starving beggar. Full-color illustrations will capture the hearts of children as they learn that sacrifice is the cornerstone for surprising blessings. This is a story that you will never forget and is sure to become a children's classic!

Tales of the Kingdom. MAINS

Back in print by popular demand, this allegorical children's classic will take you on a journey to the enchanted city as you relive the wonderful experiences of God's great deliverance. I would place this treasure on an equal with *The Chronicles of Narnia and Pilgrim's Progress.*

The True Princess. ANGELA HUNT

This book is a classic that will teach children what makes a true princess in Jesus' eyes! Truly a treasure to be passed on to the next generation. Based on the Scriptural teachings of servanthood.

The Education of a Child. FENELON

In all my years of education, I have not come across a more thorough and common sense approach to education than Francois Fenelon's treatise on education during the 17th century. Commissioned to educate King Louis XIV's grandson to prepare him for the throne, Fenelon abandoned all modern approaches to education and followed the genius of the ancient Hebrews, Egyptians, and Greeks. Fenelon believed that the ten classical virtues were the foundation for educational models and could only be taught through friendship and a gentle approach.

The Lamplighter Newsletter

Free and available upon request. Rich with biblical insights on marriage, parenting, book reviews, teaching ideas, mentoring boys and nurturing girls, and a special section devoted to "Let God's Creatures Be the Teachers."

𝕷𝖆𝖒𝖕𝖑𝖎𝖌𝖍𝖙𝖊𝖗 𝕻𝖚𝖇𝖑𝖎𝖘𝖍𝖎𝖓𝖌.

P.O. Box 777
Waverly, PA 18471
1-888-A-Gospel

e-mail: lamplighter@agospel.com
web site: www.agospel.com

Making ready a people prepared for the Lord.
Luke 1:17